The Illustrated Footballer

The Illustrated Footballer

Tony Ambrosen

BREEDON BOOKS SPORT

First published in Great Britain by
The Breedon Books Publishing Company Limited
45 Friar Gate, Derby DE1 1DA
1989

ISBN 0 907969 47 X

Printed by The Bath Press, Bath
Jacket designed by Graham Hales

CONTENTS

In the Beginning	7
The Roaring Twenties	21
The Arsenal Years	36
The Post-war Boom	47
Modern Times	57

Introduction

A HANDFUL of football cards or a few photographs can mean different things to different people. To the youngster they may be pictures of the heroes that fill up his day, to the older supporter they bring a wave of nostalgia, reminders of wet, cold winter days on terraces twenty or thirty years ago. Despite the trials and tribulations football has known — not just in recent years but throughout its existence — the game has long been the country's leading winter sport and the abiding passion of many people. It has contributed much to the social fabric of Britain and is a point of contact between young and old, rich and poor, Northerners and Southerners — and for a long time between Britain and the rest of the world. A steady stream of material has been produced to reflect this interest. Even before the days of widespread photographs, illustrations were to be found in newspapers. Since the 1890s, cards of footballers and football teams have been given away by cigarette companies and various other producers.

Much of the material now has great value, both in a financial and historical sense. Alas, we sometimes learn too late of that material worth. I well remember the cards being given away with the 'Adventure' and the 'Rover' and the black and white *Famous Footballers* in packets of Barratt's Sweet Cigarettes. The cards were thrown out or given away at a later stage and are now in many cases worth £30 or £40 a set. The financial value of such material is something of a two-edged sword for a collector, however, for while it is pleasant to feel one has a collection of some worth, inflationary costs mean that the amount of new items which can be acquired is that much more limited.

While the financial question is a debatable one, and many older collectors deplore these rising prices, it is indisputable that many of the cards and associated material have historic value, and much of this book will be taken up with discussing that aspect. Each area has its own heroes who outlive their own age. The North-East with its Milburn and Shackleton; London with its Jimmy Greaves and 'Chopper' Harris, Lancashire with Nat Lofthouse, Tom Finney and many others. The list could be continued *ad infinitum*. There is an endless stream of famous teams and famous players and one of the advantages of perusing this original material is that they can be seen without the embroidery of later generations.

Over the years hundreds of sets of football cards have been issued. Many are distinctly average, but there are numerous fine series. There are various factors which help to make a set distinctive and worth collecting, although, as with many other things, it is probably 'all in the eye of the beholder'. The most obvious qualities are good pictures and interesting biographies, where individual players are concerned. There are other factors to be considered, however, and these will be referred to throughout the book. Team photographs are particularly useful in an historical perspective, although they can be fairly useless when the names are not given. Another advantage is when more obscure players are included, for sets which include the same star players tend to become rather monotonous.

The main 'plus' qualities, however, are thought and ingenuity, for these make sets distinctive, as with the unpretentious but effective Ogden's *A.F.C. Nicknames* and Clevedon's *Football Club Managers*.

This book is not an attempt to catalogue every single series that has ever been published on the subject of football, but to show something of a panorama and to bring out the various qualities to be found in them. In recent years interest in football research has greatly increased. Cards have been used to illustrate football histories and the like and at the same time research and knowledge can help to make the study of cards more interesting. Something of the history of football is given in this book, together with the details of some of the personalities that have graced the game, in order to put the material into context.

In The Beginning

From the 1890s to World War One

IT was in the days of gaslamps and the horse and cart that the first cigarette cards rolled off the presses. Moustachioed figures in knee-length shorts and hefty boots belted an odd-looking ball around muddy fields. Queen Victoria was still on the throne and even the Boer War had not arrived, let alone the two world wars that were to devastate Europe. It would be naïve to think of it as a Golden Age, but for sure it was a different age and it is an illuminating experience, when perusing a few cards of the period, to try to recreate a mental picture of the time.

The early, monochrome heroes that look out from the cards of 'Guinea Gold' and 'Tabs' are not so very different from those of today, but it is enlightening to trace some of the more important events that led to the rise of football as a national institution, if we wish to put the production of these cards into a proper context. By the time the late-nineteenth century had arrived, football had already been played, in some form or another, for thousands of years. Indeed, it is a well-known fact that in 1365, Edward III banned the game because his bowmen were neglecting their archery practice. The game was always played on a patchwork basis, however, with anyone who desired to play seemingly eligible to participate. In the middle years of the nineteenth-century the game began to take on a more formalised nature, with an apparent desire existing to find nationally acceptable rules. The dribbling code eventually developed into soccer, as we know it today, and the handling game into rugby.

There are two major dates which signpost the way Association Football was to develop. The first was 28 October 1863, when the representatives of eleven teams met at the Freemason's Tavern in Lincoln's Inn Fields in order to establish the Football Association. This was to lead, eight years later, to the inauguaration of the FA Cup, the first season of which saw the participation of a meagre fifteen clubs, such as Great Marlow and Hampstead Heathens. In March 1888, William McGregor of Aston Villa circulated a letter to other major clubs and this led, some months later, to the foundation of the Football League. Twelve teams played in the first season, all of them coming from the North of England and the Midlands. This, then, was the background against which the earliest football cards were issued in the late 1890s. Professionalism, at first fiercely opposed by legislators, had been legalised some ten years earlier, and the foundations of soccer as a leading spectator sport had been laid. At the first FA Cup Final, only 2,000 spectators were present but the attendance for the 1895 Final at the Crystal Palace exceeded 42,000.

The first football cards to be produced were probably those in the 'Guinea Gold' series of Ogden's Limited of Liverpool, although it is unwise to be too dogmatic in the dating of cards. Over a thousand different black and white photographic cards were given away with 'Guinea Gold' and they were of general interest, covering not only football, but royalty, racehorses, actresses, railway engines and so forth. Apparently the cards were issued around the period 1894-1901 and another of Ogden's brands, 'Tabs', included a similar large series around 1900-1903. To be accurate, these are both really composite series. Various batches have slightly different format and, for the specialist, the different bases are significant.

As far as footballers are concerned, many of those included come from teams that are well-known today. Many of the original twelve have retained a prominent position in the game for a century — Aston Villa, Derby County and West Bromwich Albion, for instance, but other now obscure clubs can be found. One 'Tabs' card depicts William Butler of Druids, a team which holds a significant place in the history of Welsh soccer. They were among the prominent teams of North Wales which included, apart from Wrexham, Chirk (birthplace of Billy Meredith) and Newtown. In the early days of Welsh football, the North greatly overshadowed the South, where the game did not really get off the ground until 1910.

Even in the years around the turn of the century, there were many stars. In these two Ogden's series we can find such personalities as the Aston Villa winger, Charlie Athersmith, who on one rainy day ran down the touchline clutching a supporter's umbrella; Steve Bloomer, the immortal Derby County star who scored 352 goals in League football; and James Crabtree, who was in four League Championship-winning sides for Aston Villa. Various Scottish players are also included, such as Neil Gibson and Alec and Nick Smith of Rangers. Scottish players had long been looked on as 'professors' and had been eagerly sought as professionals (legal or otherwise), especially by Lancashire clubs.

The inclusion of Corinthians players is particularly interesting. The Corinthians had a long and distinguished existence as an amateur side, far outliving the age of 'Old Boys' and University teams that preceded the pre-Football League period. Probably the best-known Corinthian was the 'Prince of Centre-Forwards', Gilbert Oswald Smith. Always known by his initials, 'G.O.' was later a public school headmaster. Another noted Corinthian was William Oakley, who played sixteen times in the full England side and was also an international athlete.

Many of these 'Guinea Gold' and 'Tabs' were produced. They are easier to acquire than numerous sets that have been issued since and have many interesting inclusions, not least the 1899 Sheffield United FA Cup side, but viewed as a series they are pretty unwieldy. Probably the first of the football 'sets', as we know them, was the 66 *Football Series* produced by W.D. & H.O.Wills of Bristol in 1902. This set was also issued by William Clarke and Son of Liverpool and London, but the curious fact is that while the Clarke cards had biographical backs, the Will's issues advertised 'Cinderella' and 'Wild Woodbine' cigarettes. Cigarette cards were first intended as 'stiffeners' for soft packets and, because of this, early ones are often found with either blank cardboard backs or with advertisements to promote a particular brand. Biographical notes came to be the rule rather than the exception, however, and these now form a very useful fund of contemporary knowledge. A set of cards can form a 'Who's Who' of a particular period, throwing light on both the stars and more obscure figures of the era.

The Wills-Clarke set contains small (around 69 x 36mm) black and white photographs, although some have a purple hue. They show a variety of footballers, some in playing garb, others in stiff collar and tie. Many of the cards to be found at this period are very posed, often taken in photographers' studios with their characteristic props. Some Rugby Union players, such as Gwyn Nicholls, are included, but there are numerous soccer personalities of the time. R.E.Foster (Corinthians) was a Test Match cricketer and a stockbroker by profession; and Fred Forman, an international footballer, was also a draughtsman. John Cameron, who died in 1935, was with Tottenham Hotspur in a playing or managerial capacity for fourteen years. It was under him that the club won the Southern League championship and then, in 1901, became the only 'modern' non-League club to win the FA Cup. George Clawley was the goalkeeper in their Cup-winning side.

Unfortunately, with some of the sets issued in the early 1900s, even odd cards are virtually impossible to obtain. With the passage of time and increasing interest in the hobby, many items have rocketed in price or seem to have disappeared from circulation. Two sets which were once cheap, considering their age, but are now increasing in price are Ogden's 51 *Football Club Colours*, issued in May 1906, and 50 *Famous Footballers*, which came out in January, 1908. These small, coloured cards have an attractive contemporary feel about them and include such giants as 'Fatty' Foulke (no pun intended), a famous goalkeeper who, at his peak, scaled 21 stones, Jesse Pennington, the West Bromwich Albion full-back who was still playing for England in 1920, and Colin Veitch, the Newcastle United half-back and chairman of the Players' Union.

Cohen, Weenan & Co of London, a cigarette firm that in 1929 became a branch of Godfrey Phillips, produced several mixed sports series which included footballers (the earliest dating from 1898), but their all football set of 60 unnumbered *Football Captains* (1907-08) is of considerably more interest. By this period the Football League had developed two strong Divisions and the Southern League had reached the stage where it was being considered as a possible Third Division. When the Southern League was established in 1894 it consisted of sixteen clubs, including the likes of Ilford, Chatham and the Royal Ordnance Factories. By 1908 it contained teams such as Portsmouth, Southampton, Luton Town and West Ham United.

The captains of almost all the major English teams can be seen on these small, coloured cards, so that we can view representatives of long disbanded sides like Glossop North End, who once graced Division One, and Leyton, a Southern League outfit which developed Charlie Buchan. Even the colours of some teams are now strangely unfamiliar, such as Watford in their yellow, green and red bands, and Grimsby Town in their white shirts with broad red necks. An interesting inclusion in the series is Tom Hynds of Leeds City. This team was thrown out of the Football League shortly after World War One. The expulsion followed a complaint by one of their former players, Charlie Copeland, regarding under-the-counter payments in wartime matches. The remainder of their fixtures were taken over by Port Vale and not long afterwards Leeds United were set up to take the place of the old City side. Hynds, a close-season signing from Arsenal, had a short spell with Leeds City before moving on to Heart of Midlothian.

A similar series which has much appeal is 100 *Association Football Club Colours*, issued by Gallaher Ltd of Belfast and London in 1909-10. The small, coloured action figures may not be brilliant, but the degree of coverage it gives to obscure teams and players makes it both an attractive and informative series. Not only English, but Irish and Scottish teams are shown, with a brief history of the club being shown on the reverse. Where else would we see pictures of such players as C.Lynch (Derry City), David Williamson (Summerfield), C.Milnes (Rotherham County), J.Jackson (Port Glasgow), J.Magowan (Old Park Corinthians) and William Yenson (Croydon Common)? Some of these teams departed the football scene many years ago and it would be quite possible to live in the localities today without even being aware of their existence. Croydon Common, for instance, did not reappear in the Southern League after World War One, as was the case with Glossop North End, not re-elected at the Football League AGM in 1915. Some of the interesting team strips of the time include Exeter City (green with white sleeves), Huddersfield Town (maroon, with yellow hoops), Grimsby Town (maroon and blue halves) and Burnley in green. Apparently, some time after this, a woman supporter told Burnley that this colour was unlucky. The team took on the colours of Aston Villa and two years later won promotion.

Various conventional sets of famous footballers were produced around this time. These include 30 *Footballers* from J. & F.Bell of Glasgow, in 1902; and 20 *Footballers* (1904) from the Cardiff firm of Percy E.Cadle & Co. Such sets, however, are overshadowed by three long series which show us a large slice of the football scene at the time. 'Set' would be the wrong word to use to describe Taddy's *Prominent Footballers*, for it is impossible to know exactly how many were issued, yet alone manage to collect them, but we do, at least, know the contents of the Cope's sets issued with their 'Clips' and 'Solace' brands.

The name of the London-based firm of Taddy &

Co is held in awe by cigarette card collectors, with their rare series of 20 *Clowns and Circus Artistes*, in particular, attaining record-breaking prices. While their *Prominent Footballers* are not in the same price bracket, they are still valuable and are quite impressive to look at, with their sepia portraits on white backgrounds. The first two series were issued in 1907 and 1908-09 with their 'Grapnel' and 'Imperial' brands and the more valuable 'London Mixture' cards in 1913-14. The latter cards are scarcer because of the onset of World War One, and in 1920 the firm was closed down following a strike by cigarette operators, so that their excellent cards came to an end.

Some Rugby Union sides, such as Cardiff and Devonport Albion, are to be found among the *Prominent Footballers*, but most of the personalities we encounter belong to the Association code. Indeed, this is one of the few sets where contemporary officials can be found, including such notabilities as J.J.Bentley, Lord Kinnaird and William McGregor. Lord Kinnaird was himself a very famous player, appearing in the FA Cup Final on nine occasions for Wanderers and Old Etonians. He later became President of the Football Association and in 1910 was presented with the FA Cup, no less, to mark his twenty-one years in charge.

Unlike the earlier sets we have come across, these Taddy cards illustrate the first-team squads of the teams selected for inclusion, the average number of players being fifteen per side. Stars and obscurities can be found side by side. To give an example of the better-known teams, Aston Villa cards include Joe Bache, with the club for almost twenty years, William George, 'Happy' Harry Hampton and Howard Spencer. All four were English internationals and spent well over ten years playing for the club. Indeed, Spencer was a director of Villa for twenty-seven years. Some other well-known personalities include Everton's H.P.Hardman, who was a Manchester United director for almost forty years; Harry Makepeace (Everton), who also played Test cricket for England; John Fort, associated with Millwall from 1914 to the 1960s; and George Hilsdon, a prolific goalscorer with Chelsea.

Southern League sides, like New Brompton (now Gillingham) and Brighton, can be found in the series and interesting Football League sides such as Bristol City. Over the years the City have endured long periods of relative obscurity, but in the era before World War One, the team reached Division One and the FA Cup Final. Amongst the cards are members of their Cup Final side, such as Annan and Cottle, and, in particular, their England international centre-half, Billy Wedlock, previously with Aberdare.

The squad of the old Leeds City team is there. A bit of patient research can reveal an interesting picture of such sides. Among Leeds' performers are Stan Cubberley, a 1906 signing from Cliftonville and a regular for six seasons; Harry Bromage, a brilliant goalkeeper who played in the City's first Football League game; and Jimmy Freeborough, a full-back from Tottenham Hotspur. The breadth of coverage displayed in this Taddy series is such that various cards have been used to illustrate club histories and the like and a wonderful fund of contemporary football knowledge is contained.

Cope Bros & Co Ltd, a cigarette company based in Liverpool and London (most seemed to be situated in major cities), produced two football sets which are very different both to each other and to the Taddy's. The better known of the two is the series of 472 *Noted Footballers* issued with 'Clips' cigarettes. These small (63 x 35mm) black and white photographs have a distinctive blue or greenish-blue surround. In fact, two versions of the set were produced, in 1910 and 1911. Virtually all the same players (and pictures) were utilised, but a few players were replaced by others, most notably in the case of Merthyr Town, where the whole team was changed. On the back of each card is a checklist of all the players in that particular team. For some reason the Blackburn Rovers' winger 'Wee Jock' Simpson appears with a biographical as well as with a normal back. By some quirk 'Jock' was actually an England international, before the World War forced him to give up the game. One minor drawback with these 'Clips' cards is that, unlike the Taddy series, the teams are limited to nine players only. Why this odd number was chosen and not a full team squad is unclear.

Apart from Rugby Union sides (Neath, Llanelly, Ebbw Vale and so forth), some Rugby League teams, such as Oldham, are included. As far as soccer is concerned, one of the most interesting facets is the choice of Welsh clubs. As has been mentioned previously, the early cards were produced at a time when Northern teams like Chirk and Druids were dominant. In modern times we think in terms of the industrial centres, like Cardiff and Swansea, with regard to Welsh football. These teams developed late, as far as British soccer is concerned, and the ones we find in the 'Clips' series are Merthyr and Ton Pentre, who were current members of the Southern League. Clearly they employed some useful players at the time and Ton Pentre had the illustrious Moses Russell, a virtual ever-present for Wales in his later Plymouth Argyle days. In fact, in Cardiff City's first season of existence (1910-11) they were knocked out of the FA Cup by Merthyr, and the Welsh Cup by Ton Pentre.

By this period the Football League had existed for over twenty years and the old Lancashire-Midlands base of professional football had developed into a national network. Newcastle United and Sunderland had soon grown into teams of stature, as had the Sheffield clubs. We can now find, shown on the 'Clips' cards, Southern teams, such as Clapton Orient, Watford, Chelsea (elected to the Football League before they even had a side), Plymouth Argyle and Bristol City.

With the growth of the popular press, the players were no longer merely local heroes, but stars of national and even international stature. Indeed, when the great Billy Meredith had his testimonial game in 1912, even the Irish FA sent for 1,000 tickets and a crowd of almost 40,000 paid £1,400, a princely sum in those days. Soccer was now an international game, thanks to the worldwide British network of trade. It is interesting that the Empire remained fairly immune to the new mania and the main influence was on Europe and South America. In 1875, for example, the Lisbon club was founded and Oxford University visited Germany (the first overseas tour to be undertaken), and seven years later the earliest Uruguayan side was established. Association football was played at the Olympic Games, but it was well after World War One that the same kind of international competition was set up for professional football.

Apart from 'Wee Jock' Simpson and Moses Russell, all the other stars of the period are to be found on 'Clips' cards, such as Bob Crompton, a Blackburn Rovers' right-back with 41 England caps; and Charlie Roberts, a Manchester United centre-half, who was also chairman of the Players' Union.

The 'Solace' cards, issued by Cope Bros in 1909, are roughly the same size as the other set and show glazed black and white portraits of contemporary players. Not every picture is brilliant, but the set gives a valuable glimpse of the current scene. Fifteen men of every team selected were illustrated and it is remarkable that almost all of the teams concerned have remained in the top flight — Chelsea, Everton, Liverpool, Manchester United, Glasgow Celtic and so forth. This helps to underline the fact that even seventy years ago the best players and sides tended to be restricted to the big city areas.

The two Cope Bros sets and the Taddy cards all suffer from the fact that no biographical notes are to be found on the backs, but this seems to be a fact of life, that the bigger the set, the less likelihood there is to find such information, because of the effort involved. To discover anything about many of the players at this late date requires a fair amount of research. Some were internationals, such as Peter Somers, whom Glasgow Celtic re-signed from Blackburn Rovers for £120 in 1902; and William Maxwell (Bristol City), who had begun with Arbroath as an amateur in the 1890s. Some did not reach such heights, however, and their stories are lying around in old newspapers and magazines, waiting to be rediscovered.

Even before World War One, cards were issued overseas and three useful sets could be obtained from W.D & H.O. Wills' brands abroad. In September 1907, this Bristol-based firm issued 50 *Football Team Colours* with their 'Scissors' brand in India. These tasteful, coloured cards have red advertisement backs that claim 'special Army quality' and the illustrations depict fifty of the leading teams of the day. Amongst these are Burton United, who graced Division Two from 1892 to 1907, Gainsborough Trinity and Glossop North End.

A series of 67 *International Footballers* was released with Wills' 'United Service' cigarettes in November 1910. Like 'Scissors' cigarettes, 'United Service' were issued in areas were British garrisons were stationed, but the main link was not with India, but with the Channel Islands. The small (59 x 35mm) black and white photographs show many of the leading performers of the day. The one short-coming of the series is that some of the internationals are attributed to the wrong country, so that A.Aitken, W.C.Davies and W.Lacey are shown as being England 'caps', although they played for Scotland, Wales and Ireland respectively.

Like many of the other sets of the era, *International Footballers* has a character all its own. Although, strictly speaking, the cards lack biographical backs, the basic facts are given, so that we can discover, for instance, that R.E.Evans of Wales was 24, stood 5ft 11in tall, weighed 11st 10lb, and played for Saltney Carriage Works, Wrexham and Aston Villa.

Despite the fact that some of the players are still well-known today, such as Billy Meredith, Andy Ducat and Charlie Thomson, others are less so. Alex Higgins of Newcastle United and Scotland was the son of another Scottish international of the same name. Typical of the forgotten 'names' are F.Thompson (Cliftonville) and the two Welsh internationals Evan Jones, who was restricted to just over twenty first-team games with Chelsea, and E.Peake of Liverpool.

The *International Footballers* series was also issued with 'Flag' cigarettes and the third 'Scissors' set can be found with a different back too. It is rather more run-of-the-mill than the other two sets, but still quite acceptable. 50 *Famous Footballers* was released in September, 1914 and unfortunately the limited colours used give the portraits a rather drab look. The cards are standard size (64 x 35mm) and the selection of players has a distinct Lancashire bias. Personalities such as Tommy Boyle, Edwin Mosscrop and Bert Freeman of the 1914 Burnley Cup-winning side can be seen, as well as Bill Lacey, John Sheldon and Arthur Metcalf of the defeated Liverpool team. It was Freeman who scored the only goal of the match.

One of the most prized names of pre-World War One cigarette card producers is that of F. & J.Smith, a Glasgow firm. Fortunately, the company published several fine series of football cards. In 1906, a set of 120 *Footballers* (brown backs) was produced, but these are, sadly, rarely seen and extremely costly. Two other sets are quite scarce and have increased greatly in price over the last few years, but 'odds' of them are rather more commonly found. The untitled 1908 series of footballers (blue backs) is strangely numbered. The top number is 104, but four cards were apparently unissued, so that we are left with a round 100. The other set of 150 *Footballers* was put out in November 1914.

The unnumbered set, with 'Cup-tie' backs (ten for twopence half-penny), is typical of the Smith cards in its bias towards Scottish footballers. It is not without a fair sprinkling of other stars, however, with players such as Billy Meredith, Alf Common — whose £1,000 transfer to Middlesbrough in February 1905 created a sensation and brought about the introduction of the transfer deadline — and the Reverend K.R.G. Hunt, who won an FA Cup winner's medal with Wolves in 1908 and an Amateur Cup winner's medal with Oxford City in 1913.

Some of the Scottish players in the set, such as Henry Collins, the Falkirk left-half, and J.H.Rattray, the Motherwell full-back, were never 'capped'.

There is a pleasing selection of Scottish internationals of the period, however, with players like Alex Smith (Rangers), William Lennie (Aberdeen) and Bill Muir, the Heart of Midlothian goalkeeper. One of the most interesting inclusions is Robert Cumming, the Greenock Morton centre-forward. In fact, his association with Morton was very brief and he was best known as a player for Glasgow Rangers, for whom he had two spells. He was a schoolmaster by profession, having gained an MA at Glasgow University, and became Lord Provost of that city in 1931.

Two other cigarette manufacturers of interest in a football context are W.A. & A.C.Churchman of Ipswich, and Murray, Sons & Co Ltd of Belfast. The latter, although never one of the biggest firms, issued a few dozen sets of cards over a forty-year period. In 1912, Murray's brought out 34 *Footballers* (Series H) and the following year, 104 (Series J). the backs of their cards advertised their brands, including 'Front-Bench' cigarettes and 'Egyptian Sunbeams'. These small (67 x 36mm) black and white portraits comprised a reasonable selection of the better-known players of the day, including Billy Meredith, Steve Bloomer, Frank Cuggy who was a well-respected name in Sunderland, and Harold Halse who played in FA Cup Finals with Manchester United, Aston Villa and Chelsea. Some Irish players are also included, such as S.Burnison and Leo Donnelly (Distillery), P.McCann (Glentoran) and F.McKee (Belfast Celtic).

Churchman's produced a vast number of cigarette cards over a long period. Two series issued in the pre-World War One era were their 50 *Footballers* (with Inset) in November, 1914 and their 50 brown *Footballers* (Photogravure), which came out at roughly the same time. The former set is quite attractive, with all the cards showing coloured match action, with a black and white portrait in an oval. It is indicative of the strength of the Southern League at this time that quite a few of the players came from this quarter. These include A.Mitchell (Queen's Park Rangers), H.Colclough (Crystal Palace) who was an England international who retired through wartime injury, and Walter Otto Davis, a Millwall Athletic centre-forward who played five times for Wales.

The photogravure series of sepia portraits is very scarce and, like other sets of the time, was probably curtailed by the onset of the war. Unlike modern cards, virtually all cards of this period were designed to fit in cigarette packets. The content of this photogravure set has an odd sort of bias, not only towards East Anglia (because of the geographical situation), but also the North-East. The set includes such players as Billy Hampson and the goalscorer Cecil Potter of Norwich City and 'Geordie' Holley, Jackie Mordue and Charlie Thomson of the illustrious Sunderland side.

Virtually all the cards we have reviewed in this chapter were issued by cigarette companies. The trade issues which we shall come across in later periods were almost non-existent, certainly as regards football, and the only inserts distributed by boys' periodicals that come to mind are the three *Famous Footballers* which came out with the 'Boy Friend' in December 1911. We have not looked at every single football card issued in the pre-1918 era, many of which are both extremely expensive and hardly ever seen. Two others which are worth referring to are the one-club series issued by the Northampton firm J.Lees and Jones Bros of Tottenham.

The 1915 Lees set consisted of twenty-one Northampton Town footballers, including the Welsh international, E.Lloyd Davies. The cards were very well produced, with the surrounds in maroon to match the club colours. Reproductions of the Jones cards have recently been issued, so that they are now accessible to the collector of more modest means. The set is restricted solely to Tottenham Hotspur players, the club having made its name in 1901, as the only Southern League side to win the FA Cup. It was only in 1908 that Spurs joined the Football League. These three-quarter-length black and white shots, although slightly rough in their reproduction, are a worthwhile addition to any collection and show such players as Ernie Coquet, signed from Reading in 1908, John Curtis and T.H.Lunn. The cards were issued around 1911.

In addition to cigarette cards, quite a quantity of postcards were produced about this period. To cover these is beyond the scope of this book, especially since many of them seem to have been local in character. However, one field that is worthy of discussion and has been sadly neglected is that of the team photographs given away with newspapers. These items turn up from time to time on lists and in auctions and can often be obtained for more reasonable sums than vintage cigarette cards. Newspapers, such as the 'Daily Citizen', the 'Sunday Chronicle' and 'Lloyds News' and magazines such as 'Ideas' (E.Hulton & Co Ltd) gave away excellent large photographs. These now have great historic interest, with their team groups of many decades ago.

The 'Daily Citizen' supplements of 1913-14 are particularly attractive sepia photographs. It is possible to detect in team pictures of this period a kind of hierarchy, with the chairman in his bowler, the manager in his straw boater, and the trainer in his flat cap. Some of the interesting teams included in this series are Belfast Celtic, Newport County (then in the Second Division of the Southern League and struggling to continue) and Cardiff City, with a young Fred Keenor and Billy Hardy, both destined to play a major role in the fine City side of the 1920s.

The historical value of such supplements is well illustrated by the 'Sunday Chronicle' series. Apart from old photographs of such teams as Blackpool and Sheffield Wednesday, we find Gainsborough Trinity in their Second Division days and Burton United in their final League season. It would be extremely difficult to find similar photographs from this period from any other source. Apart from this, the pictures have a quaint, naïve charm about them, with the trainer's towel draped over his shoulder and the odd player's bicycle parked in the distance.

Various other items of football interest can be found from this period. Buttonhole badges with the colours of different teams were given away by

A WELSH ASSOCIATION TEAM.

Some pictures of the newly-formed Cardiff City F.C., which nas taken the Association code into the very stronghold of the Rugby game—Cardiff. What is more, they draw an average crowd of 20,000 spectators. Cardiff City is taking part in the Second Division of the Southern League, as the stepping-stone, presumably, to higher things.

1. A view of the Cardiff City ground, which is destined to become one of the most popular football resorts in the country.
2. A tussle in front of goal.
3. The toss-up for choice of ends.
4. The Cardiff City team (from left to right). Top row: Messrs. F. Burfitt and Councillor Wall (Directors), Duffy, Mackenzie, Husbands, Abley, Nash, Messrs. Nicholls and Eveleigh (Directors). Middle row: Malloch, Powell, Laurie, Ramsey, and Macdonald. Bottom row: S. Nicholls, Stewart, Peake, and Ewen.
5. Cardiff City's mascot, a typical Welsh goat.

cigarette producers.

Magazines like 'Football Chat' and 'Lottinga's Weekly' were published and these reflect the popular interest in the sport at that time. Certainly on one occasion the Southern League brought out a book of team photographs (the 'Southern Football League Portrait Album'), where teams like Queen's Park Rangers, Portsmouth, Southampton and West Ham United can be seen in their pre-Football League days.

With the onset of World War One, football as an organised spectator sport began to run down. The initial hopes for a short struggle in Europe soon proved ill-founded and after the end of the 1914-15 season many clubs went into limbo, with the remainder operating in less competitive, regional leagues. The importance of football clearly diminished in the face of the increasing slaughter of the war, and the needs of the war-effort meant the curtailment of card issues.

Although the issue of cards seems to have died out after about 1914, one set has, in fact, been attributed to 1917 and this is the extremely attractive and interesting F. & J.Smith set of 50 *Football Club Records.* The fronts are coloured portraits in an oval and the backs show the latest record of the club in question — these vary from 1913-14 to 1916-17, since teams ceased playing at various periods. The interest of the subject matter lies in two factors. In the first place, the Scottish First Division sides are included, rather than just the English sides, so that we may see players such as H.Dainty (Ayr United), W.McAndrew (Clyde) and J.G.Rowan (Dumbarton). One particularly colourful character is Donald Colman of Aberdeen. His real name was Cunningham, but he adopted another so that his disapproving father would not discover his involvement with soccer. He did not enter the first-class game until the age of twenty-seven and later became a trainer, coaching in Norway in the summer. He was responsible for the introduction of the trainer's dugout. The other curiosity lies in the fact that many of the players are stated to be 'OHMS', since they were in the armed services. In the case of the unfortunate E.S.Garvie of Queen's Park we may even find the comment underneath 'died of wounds....'

A selection of scarce cards from the pre-1914 era.

Early Ogdens, c1900. The captions for Billy Bassett and Jackie Robertson are transposed.

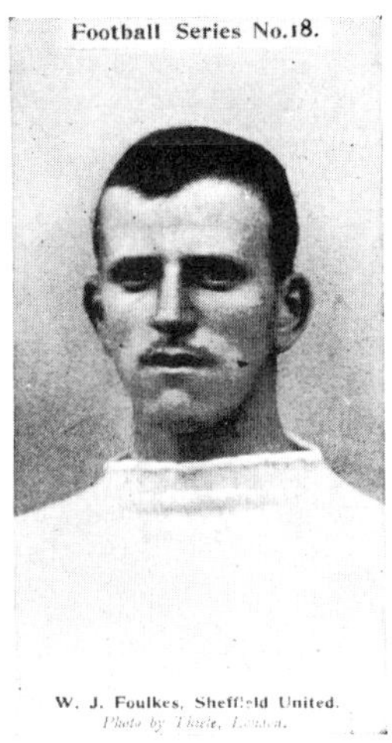

Wills Footballers 1901.

Smith's Cup Tie Footballers, c1908.

Ogden's 'Football Club Colours' (1906).

Wills' Scissors 'Football Club Colours' (1907).

Ogden's 'Famous Footballers' (1908).

Cohen Weenan's 'Football Captains' (1908).

Gallaher's 'Association Football Club Colours' (1910).

Gallaher's 'Association Football Club Colours' (1910).

Cope's Clips 'Noted Footballers' (1910).

Churchman's 'Footballers' with inset (1914).

FOOTBALL CLUB RECORDS.
A SERIES OF 50.—No. 47

WEST BROMWICH ALBION.
Winners of F. A. Cup, 1888, 1892.
Runners up, 1886, 1887, 1895, 1912.
ENGLISH LEAGUE, DIV. I.,
RECORD 1914-5.

	Home.	Away.
Blackburn Rov.	D 0—0	L 1—2
Aston Villa ..	W 2—0	L 1—2
Middlesbrough ..	W 1—0	L 0—2
Oldham Athletic	D 0—0	D 1—1
Bolton Wand. ..	W 3—0	D 1—1
Sunderland ..	L 1—2	W 2—1
Chelsea	W 2—0	L 1—4
Bradford City ..	W 3—0	L 0—5
Sheffield United	D 1—1	L 0—2
Newcastle United	W 2—0	W 2—1
Burnley	W 3—0	W 2—0
Manchester City	L 0—1	L 0—4
Everton	L 1—2	L 1—2
Liverpool.. ..	W 4—0	L 1—3
Tottenham H. ..	W 3—2	L 0—2
Sheffield Wed. ..	D 0—0	D 0—0
Bradford	W 1—0	W 4—1
Manchester Unit.	D 0—0	D 0—0
Notts County ..	W 4—1	D 1—1

Total played, 38: W., 15; L., 13; D., 10. Goals for, 49; against, 43. Points, 40. Position, 11th.

Issued by The Imperial Tobacco Co. (of Great Britain & Ireland), Limited.

FOOTBALL CLUB RECORDS.
A SERIES OF 50.—No. 40

PORTSMOUTH.
SOUTHERN LEAGUE.
Champions, 1902.
LONDON COMBN., RECORD 1916-7.

	Home.	Away.
West Ham United	L 1—2	L 1—5
Millwall	L 0—1	L 0—2
Tottenham H. ..	L 2—4	L 1—2
Chelsea	W 2—1	L 0—6
Fulham	L 3—4	L 0—9
Woolwich Arsenal	W 1—0	L 0—1
Luton	L 0—4	D 2—2
Southampton ..	L 0—1	L 1—2
Crystal Palace ..	D 2—2	L 3—5
Watford	W 3—0	L 0—1
Queen's Park R.	L 2—3	W 7—1
Brentford.. ..	L 0—2	L 0—7
Clapton Orient ..	W 2—0	D 1—1
West Ham United	L 2—5	L 2—5
Tottenham H. ..	L 2—4	L 0-10
Southampton ..	W 1—0	L 0—1
Crystal Palace ..	L 1—2	W 3—2
Watford	W 8—3	L 0—9
Clapton Orient ..	W 3—0	L 1—6
Woolwich Arsenal	(N.pl.)	L 1—2

Total played, 39; W., 9; L., 27; D., 3. Goals for, 58; against, 117. Points, 21. Position, 13th.

Issued by The Imperial Tobacco Co. (of Great Britain & Ireland), Limited.

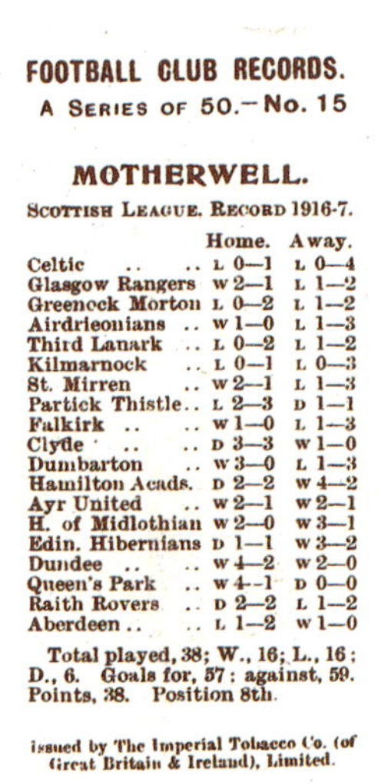

FOOTBALL CLUB RECORDS.
A SERIES OF 50.—No. 15

MOTHERWELL.
SCOTTISH LEAGUE. RECORD 1916-7.

	Home.	Away.
Celtic	L 0—1	L 0—4
Glasgow Rangers	W 2—1	L 1—2
Greenock Morton	L 0—2	L 1—2
Airdrieonians ..	W 1—0	L 1—3
Third Lanark ..	L 0—2	L 1—2
Kilmarnock ..	L 0—1	L 0—3
St. Mirren ..	W 2—1	L 1—3
Partick Thistle..	L 2—3	D 1—1
Falkirk	W 1—0	L 1—3
Clyde	D 3—3	W 1—0
Dumbarton ..	W 3—0	L 1—3
Hamilton Acads.	D 2—2	W 4—2
Ayr United ..	W 2—1	W 2—1
H. of Midlothian	W 2—0	W 3—1
Edin. Hibernians	D 1—1	W 3—2
Dundee	W 4—2	W 2—0
Queen's Park ..	W 4—1	D 0—0
Raith Rovers ..	D 2—2	L 1—2
Aberdeen	L 1—2	W 1—0

Total played, 38; W., 16; L., 16; D., 6. Goals for, 57: against, 59. Points, 38. Position 8th.

Issued by The Imperial Tobacco Co. (of Great Britain & Ireland), Limited.

F. & J.Smith's 'Football Club Records' (1917).

F. & J. SMITH'S CIGARETTES

CLYDE.
W. MCANDREW.
O.H.M.S.

FOOTBALL CLUB RECORDS.
A SERIES OF 50.—No. 8

EDINBURGH HIBERNIANS.
Winners Scottish Cup, 1887, 1902.
SCOTTISH LEAGUE.
Champions, 1903.
SCOTTISH LEAGUE, RECORD 1916-7.

	Home.	Away.
Celtic	L 0—1	L 1—3
Glasgow Rangers	D 0—0	L 1—5
Greenock Morton	L 2—4	D 1—1
Airdrieonians ..	D 1—1	L 1—3
Third Lanark ..	D 1—1	D 1—1
Kilmarnock ..	W 2—1	W 3—1
St. Mirren ..	W 2—1	D 1—1
Motherwell ..	L 2—3	D 1—1
Partick Thistle..	W 1—0	W 3—0
Falkirk	L 1—2	W 1—0
Clyde	D 1—1	W 2—1
Dumbarton ..	W 3—1	L 1—2
Hamilton Acads.	W 4—3	L 2—4
Ayr United ..	L 1—4	L 1—2
H. of Midlothian	L 0—2	L 0—2
Dundee	L 1—2	L 1—3
Queen's Park ..	W 5—1	L 1—4
Raith Rovers ..	D 3—3	L 1—2
Aberdeen.. ..	D 3—3	L 1—2

Total played, 38; W., 10; L., 18; D., 10. Goals for, 57; against, 72. Points, 30. Position, 17th.

Issued by The Imperial Tobacco Co. (of Great Britain & Ireland), Limited.

F. & J. SMITH'S CIGARETTES

DUMBARTON.
J. G. ROWAN,
O.H.M.S.

F. & J. SMITH'S CIGARETTES

GREENOCK MORTON.
J. S. WRIGHT.

F. & J. SMITH'S CIGARETTES

AIRDRIEONIANS.
J. REID,
O.H.M.S.

F. & J. SMITH'S CIGARETTES

QUEEN'S PARK.
E. S. GARVIE,
DIED OF WOUNDS.

F. & J. SMITH'S CIGARETTES

THIRD LANARK.
J. BROWNLIE,
O.H.M.S.

FOOTBALL CLUB RECORDS.
A SERIES OF 50.—No. 3

AYR UNITED.
SCOTTISH LEAGUE, RECORD 1916-7.

	Home.	Away.
Celtic	L 0—1	L 0—5
Glasgow Rangers	L 1—3	L 0—1
Greenock Morton	L 0—3	L 0—2
Airdrieonians ..	D 1—1	L 0—1
Third Lanark ..	L 0—1	L 3—4
Kilmarnock ..	L 0—2	W 2—1
St. Mirren ..	W 2—1	D 0—0
Motherwell ..	L 1—2	L 1—2
Partick Thistle..	D 0—0	L 0—3
Falkirk	D 2—2	W 2—1
Clyde	D 1—1	W 4—1
Dumbarton ..	W 3—1	L 1—3
Hamilton Acads.	D 1—1	L 1—2
H. of Midlothian	W 2—0	W 2—1
Edin. Hibernians	W 2—1	W 4—1
Dundee	L 1—2	L 1—2
Queen's Park ..	D 1—1	L 2—3
Raith Rovers ..	W 2—1	W 3—1
Aberdeen.. ..	W 1—0	L 0—1

Total played, 38; W., 12; L., 19; D., 7. Goals for, 47; against, 59. Points, 31. Position, 15th.

Issued by The Imperial Tobacco Co. (of Great Britain & Ireland), Limited.

FOOTBALL CLUB RECORDS.
A SERIES OF 50.—No. 10

GLASGOW RANGERS.
Winners of Scottish Cup, 1894, 1897, 1898, 1903.
SCOTTISH LEAGUE.
Champions, 1891, 1899, 1900, 1901, 1902, 1911, 1912, and 1913.
SCOTTISH LEAGUE, RECORD 1916-7.

	Home.	Away.
Celtic	D 0—0	D 0—0
Greenock Morton	L 0—1	L 0—1
Airdrieonians ..	W 3—0	L 0—2
Third Lanark ..	L 0—2	D 1—1
Kilmarnock ..	W 3—0	L 1—4
St. Mirren ..	W 1—0	D 1—1
Motherwell ..	W 2—1	L 1—2
Partick Thistle..	W 3—0	W 1—0
Falkirk	W 3—1	W 3—0
Clyde	W 1—0	W 1—0
Dumbarton ..	W 6—0	W 2—0
Hamilton Acads.	W 2—0	L 1—3
Ayr United ..	W 1—0	W 3—1
H. of Midlothian	W 1—0	W 3—1
Edin. Hibernians	W 5—1	D 0—0
Dundee	W 3—0	L 1—2
Queen's Park ..	W 1—0	W 4—1
Raith Rovers ..	W 4—3	W 4—1
Aberdeen ..	W 1—0	L 1—3

Total played, 38; W., 24; L., 9; D., 5. Goals for, 68; against, 32. Points, 53. Position, 3rd.

Issued by The Imperial Tobacco Co. (of Great Britain & Ireland), Limited.

F. & J. SMITH'S CIGARETTES

HAMILTON ACADEMICALS.
J. WATSON,
O.H.M.S.

F. & J. SMITH'S CIGARETTES

ABERDEEN.
D. COLMAN.
O.H.M.S.

F. & J. SMITH'S CIGARETTES

CELTIC.
A. MCNAIR.

F. & J.Smith's 'Football Club Records' (1917).

J. WHITE.
HEART OF MIDLOTHIAN.

W. RANKIN.
MOTHERWELL.

T. TOWNSLEY.
FALKIRK.

F. WALKER.
THIRD LANARK.

E. TAYLOR.
HUDDERSFIELD TOWN.

J. McDOUGALL.
AIRDRIEONIANS.

J. HUTTON.
ABERDEEN.

GEO. HENDERSON.
RANGERS.

J. H. RAMSAY.
KILMARNOCK.

H. RITCHIE.
HIBERNIANS.

L. McMILLAN.
HAMILTON ACADEMICALS.

D. LAWSON.
ST. MIRREN.

J.Filshill's 'Footballers' (1924).

Gallaher's mixed 'Famous Footballers' (late 1920s).

Gallaher's mixed action shots (late 1920s).

Ogden's 'Captains of Association Football Club & Colours' (1926).

Player's 'Footballers, Caricatures by Rip' (1926).

Player's 'Football Caricatures, by Mac' (1927).

Taddy's Footballers, c1908.

Cope's "Solace" 1910.

Wills 'Scissors' International Footballers, c1910.

Churchman's sepia, c1914.

The Roaring Twenties
After World War One

THE carnage of what was then known as the Great War could not persist forever and in 1918 it thankfully drew to a close. Clearly, the holocaust must have left an imprint on the mind of everybody, but the only positive approach now was to try and forget the past and build a new future. Many things had likewise changed in football and many individuals would not return to the field. Evelyn Lintott, for instance, was killed on the Somme in 1916 and 'Sandy' Turnbull, star of both Manchester clubs, died in France in May 1917. Jimmy Spiers, who scored the 1911 FA Cup Final winner for Bradford City, lost his life in 1917. Others received lasting injuries, though Jimmy Seed, for one, overcame a gassing to find football fame. Some teams had also disappeared, like Glossop North End in Division Two and Croydon Common in the Southern League.

With the desire for a new beginning came the reorganisation of the Football League. The idea of creating a Third Division from the Southern League had been mooted for years and this was implemented in 1920, followed a year later by the establishment of the Third Division North. In Scotland the situation was more confused. At first there was a delay in the re-establishing of the Second Division, but by the mid-1920s there were, for several seasons, three Divisions.

Just as things had altered on the field of play, so things had changed in the world of card production. Before the war almost all cards had been released by cigarette producers. Boys' magazines began to put out many cards in their circulation battle and other firms, particularly in the confectionery business, produced similar material. These issues are known to collectors as 'trade cards' and they were, for many years, looked down on as being in some way inferior to cigarette cards. Things have changed in recent years, however, possibly as the percentage of the population that actually collected cigarette cards out of the packets has decreased. Scarce trade cards can command high prices and, in truth, there is probably not a great deal of difference in the standard of cigarette and trade cards. Both include good and bad sets, interesting and tedious, colourful and drab.

The last set that was mentioned in the pre-1918 period was F. & J.Smith's *Football Club Records* and here we have a link with that era, for in 1922 the same firm put out a second and equally attractive set of 50 *Football Club Records*, covering the 1921-22 season. Again each card consisted of a neat, colourful portrait in an oval, with the team's playing record on the reverse. Three Welsh Rugby Union sides are included, but all of the other cards show soccer players. As with the other F. & J.Smith football series, there is a prominent Scottish League presence and there are 21 cards representing Scottish League sides, where we may see such personalities as William Reid, the Albion Rovers' player-manager, R.Orrock (Alloa Athletic) and William Collier (Raith Rovers), who had not started playing football until joining the Army at the age of twenty-five.

Whether in every case it was the team captain who was selected for these Smith's cards is difficult to establish, but certainly these issues, apart from showing a variety of players, give an excellent picture of each team's current playing strip. Some of the English performers were real stars of the time, such as Joe Smith, whose nineteen goal-scoring years for Bolton Wanderers were followed by an equally successful twenty-three years as Blackpool manager, and Bob Kelly, who spent over twenty years in League soccer.

Another quite different, but equally attractive series had been issued around two years previously. About this time many 'silks' were produced, ie. pictures woven in silk with a paper backing sheet. These enjoyed considerable popularity and there were even competitions to make patchwork quilts out of them. Although many of these silks were issued, only one series devoted to a football theme appeared and this was Godfrey Phillips' BDV *Football League Colours*. This London company released several dozen series of unbacked silks between 1910 and 1925 and this particular one dates from 1920, just after the introduction of the Third Division. The cards came in two sizes, small (68 x 48mm) and extra-large (150 x 100mm) and were not just restricted to soccer, for many of the bright Rugby League strips are included.

Not all of the soccer colours in the series are familiar to us. Fulham are shown in green and Bury in red and white stripes, for instance, and some of the colours may, in fact, be questionable. Newport County are represented by light-blue shirts, but they were never recorded as wearing these, although they did briefly, in time of post-war shortage, wear old shirts donated by West Bromwich Albion. Whatever the limitations, however, these silks add an extra dimension to a collection, with their unusual quality and vibrant colours.

From the historical viewpoint, there is one series which dominates all the others from this period, the *Pinnace Footballers* produced by the same company, Godfrey Phillips Ltd. Although the vast majority are merely miniature (45 x 35mm) black and white portraits, with no information on the backs, there were 2,462 issued, covering all of the main players of the time and these cards have been used profusely, in recent years, to illustrate club histories and similar publications.

The date which has been given for this *Pinnace* series is 1922 and it has been linked with the opening of Wembley Stadium. The cards were issued over several years, however, and the date for the original issues must have been earlier. Two Newport County players, for instance, Jackie Mann and 'Pat' Collins (an FA Cup winner with Wolverhampton Wanderers) did not play for the club after April 1920 and had left by the time the new Third Division commenced in September 1920. Since there has always been a desperate effort on producers' part to ensure players' teams are up to date, we may assume that the first cards were issued around the start of the 1920-21 season.

There is no great pattern to be found in the way that the *Pinnace* cards are arranged. As stated previously, they were issued over several years and, indeed, the backs can be found in five different formats. The early cards were produced in batches of four per club, although this became less obvious as players were transferred. Later ones, however, were produced more or less in first-team squads. The normal cards were miniature size, but, as the backs reveal, a cabinet-sized photograph could be received in exchange for twenty-five small ones, a team group for 100 and large cards could be obtained in packets of 50 cigarettes. The larger issues are obviously much more difficult to obtain today. Two different styles of album were produced for the cards. The one had eleven sets of slots per sheet, so that the best side could be selected for each club.

The *Pinnace* collection does not merely consist of Football League performers. Apart from a dozen Welsh Rugby Union players, many Rugby Leaguers are included. Many of the latter can be found in two versions — with NU and RFL after the teams, as this was the period when the name was changed from Northern Union (which had existed since the breakaway over broken-time payments) to Rugby Football League. This is the only large scale issue of pre-war Rugby League players, although quite a few were produced by the 'News Chronicle' in the 1950s. There are also a great number of Scottish Division One performers, which is a great boon to any historian of those clubs, and, most interestingly, there are many players from the amateur Isthmian League, including such teams as Ilford and Nunhead. Information from this period of football history abounds, notably through the good offices of the late, lamented 'Athletic News', which included reports on every weekend game in its weekly issues and put out annuals giving appearances and goalscorers and players' heights, weights and birthplaces.

As far as the Football League teams are concerned, one of the fascinations is with the number of defunct clubs to be found in the series. Not only can we see sides that have fairly recently left the League, such as Barrow and Southport, but also the likes of Aberdare Athletic, Durham City (who produced England players George Camsell and Sammy Crooks), Ashington (home of the Milburn clan), and Stalybridge Celtic who, after two seasons of League membership, decided to drop out. It is easy to look disparagingly on such teams, but during their period of membership they were on a par with other sides and had many experienced players on their books. The main reason why teams left the Football League at this time was economic — the general slump led to poor attendances and this, in turn, meant the selling of better players. The geographical position of the clubs is significant, with Ashington and Durham City in the North-East; Aberdare Athletic, Merthyr Town and, briefly, Newport County in South Wales; and Stalybridge Celtic, Nelson and Wigan Borough in the North-West. The fact is that the Third Divisions were launched at completely the wrong moment. The high hopes which followed the ending of the war soured as the General Strike was accompanied by the Depression of the 1920s and 1930s. In Scotland, the 'C' Division was abandoned as clubs could no longer meet their commitments.

The *Pinnace* photographs, as stated previously, have been of great assistance in the compilation of club histories and similar publications and a study of a couple of teams' players may help to illustrate how much can be contributed by a bit of research. Let us take some of the players used by Aberdare Athletic and Merthyr Town as an example. Many of the Merthyr performers left the club after a short spell, mostly being sold to keep the Town going. Albert Langford, for instance, a very useful right-back, went to Swansea Town for £600 in 1923. Dai Nicholas, a winger, joined Stoke a year earlier before likewise moving to Swansea. In 1922, Willie Walker went to Bristol City, the goalscoring George Beel to Chesterfield and Jennings to Luton Town. Others on the move in the next season or two included the Foxall brothers, together again at Portsmouth, and Evan Edwards, an amateur international winger who joined Wolverhampton Wanderers. The most interesting of the characters shown is the goalkeeper, Albert Lindon. He had three spells at Merthyr and managed that club and Charlton Athletic. He was assistant manager at Cardiff City some thirty years later and had a spell as Arsenal scout.

Although soccer had been played in Aberdare since the turn of the century, the Athletic had a very brief history. Formed after World War One, they had only one season in the Welsh League before being elected to the Third Division South. After six seasons in the Football League they lost out to Torquay United on a second ballot for re-election and were wound up the following year. During their League career they employed many experienced players. James Martin, for instance, was a professional for over fifteen years and his clubs included Stoke, Reading and Bristol City. Colin Myers was a talented inside-right who played for Bradford City, Northampton Town and Queen's Park Rangers. After his spell with the Athletic, the impressive goalkeeper Joe Duckworth spent six seasons with Reading, and Tom Mayson had been Grimsby Town's record signing when they bought him for over £300 in 1911. W.Lot Jones was another colourful character. After starting his career with Chirk and Druids, he moved to Manchester City, where he made 279 League appearances in eleven years. A dazzling footballer at his best, he amassed twenty caps for Wales when many less games were played than today. He continued his career to the veteran stage and eventually ended up back with Chirk.

These two old Welsh clubs have simply been chosen as examples and no doubt all of the other clubs included in this great series have similar, interesting tales to tell. The cards make accessible to us players who would otherwise be simply names on a list. Fortunately, a book entitled *The Pinnace Collection* was issued in 1986 and this included reproductions of all the cards in the series. Apart from the obvious advantage of seeing cards which are, in some cases, unobtainable and, in bulk, expensive, another virtue is that the teams are given for players whose names alone are printed on the card. Although the early cards were printed with team names, some of the higher numbered cards either had the team name literally stuck on the back or simply identified the player. Whatever the minor shortcomings we can find with this series, anyone interested in football history studies it and uses it.

The London firm of R. & J. Hill Ltd brought out another football set in 1923 with its 50 *Famous Footballers*. This is in complete contrast to the *Pinnace* series, being in number, size and content an entirely conventional set. The fronts hold distinctive, if somewhat muted, sepia portraits and the biographical backs have attractive green and brown artwork, including an advertisement for 'Sunripe' cigarettes. There is a London bias in the selection of these post-war players, amongst whom we find Alf Capper, the Brentford right-winger, A.A.Goodman, the Charlton Athletic centre-forward who later joined Gillingham, L.G.Hill, the Queen's Park Rangers goalkeeper later with Southampton, and Charlie Alton, the Brentford full-back.

The set of 50 *Football Teams* put out with 'Islanders Fags' in the 1923-4 season is curious, for, although the firm of Bucktrout and Co Ltd was a Guernsey associate of BAT, the teams in the set were all well-known British outfits. The colours of these medium-sized cards (69 x 48mm) are somewhat drab, an unfortunate feature of many of the sets from this period, but the backs name all of the players, a great advantage to anyone interested in the team or the era. Some of the clubs no longer enjoy the prominent position they once held. We can see pictures of Cardiff City, an impressive team at the time with Farquharson, Fred Keenor and Billy Hardy; South Shields, who later became Gateshead; and Clapton Orient, who, after World War Two, became Leyton Orient and restored the Leyton prefix in 1987 after several years as just plain Orient. The Bristol City card features their manager, Alec Raisbeck, who can be seen as a player in some of the earliest football series.

Between 1923 and 1925, the British American Tobacco Co Ltd issued three sets of 50 *Famous Footballers* overseas. Despite the washed-out grey and buff colours, the selection of footballers and the biographical backs make them worthwhile to the collector. Amongst the players shown are such personalities as Jack Evans and Len Davies, noted Welsh internationals with Cardiff City; Harold Fleming, Swindon Town's England 'cap', who had been destined for the Church; and David Brown, Darlington's Scottish centre-forward, who amassed 39 goals in 1924-5. Others, like Notts County's giant goalkeeper Albert Iremonger, Sam Hardy (Liverpool) and Frank Hudspeth (Newcastle United) show the depth of talent around in the football world at this time.

The Manchester firm of J.A.Pattreiouex, later a part of Gallaher Ltd, produced various sets of interest to the football follower. Hundreds of photographic cards of footballers were produced around the mid 1920s. This was really a composite set, with series lettered F, FA, FB and FC, which suggests that the cards were issued over a considerable period. The picture quality is rather monotonous — black and white with a brownish tinge — and the selection of photographs is somewhat peculiar, but there is such a wealth of material that the set is very collectable. Most of the cards are concerned with soccer, but one can find the Welsh and Irish Rugby Union sides and, on FC60, HRH The Prince of Wales with his topper and binoculars. Some of the cards have very brief notes on the reverse and others merely an advertisement for 'Casket' and 'Trawler' cigarettes. Some action shots are included, with such scenes as Bury in training and Bowser leading out West Bromwich Albion, and on another we can find the Middlesbrough forward line. There are some team groups included in the series, but, unfortunately, not all have the players listed on the reverse.

Two non-photographic series of 50 and 100 *Famous Footballers* were produced by Pattreiouex around 1927, having coloured portraits on brown backgrounds. The set of 50 is identified by its blue captions, the other having brown. There is a distinct Lancashire presence on the cards. The famous Bolton Wanderers side, which won the FA Cup three times in seven years, is represented by such stalwarts as Harry Nuttall, Jimmy Seddon and Bill Jennings and other favourites from Lancashire include Charlie Pringle, the Scottish wing-half of Manchester City; Jack Silcock of Manchester United; and Ron Sewell, the Blackburn Rovers goalkeeper.

Gallaher Ltd, of Belfast and London, produced four excellent sets around this period, namely 100 *Footballers* (Red Back) in 1928, 50 *Famous Footballers* (Brown Back) in 1926, 100 *Famous Footballers* (Green Back) in 1925 and 50 *Footballers in Action* (Blue Back) in 1928. The cards have a characteristic quality about them and are sized around 62 x 37mm. The geographical situation of Gallaher Ltd give the green-back series a distinctive Irish quality and we can find such forgotten heroes as Harold Burnison, the Distillery left-back, Sam Moore, the Belfast Celtic right-half, and Joe Mehaffy, New Brighton's Irish goalkeeper.

The red-back series really consists of two distinct sets, the first of match action shots, the second of coloured portraits. The date of these cards has been given as 1925 — puzzling, as the 1928 FA Cup Final is included. In fact, the dates attributed to many football series are wrong, as a scrutiny of the subject matter will confirm. The action pictures in this particular set certainly have a curiosity value and we may see Darlington versus Bradford (Park Avenue) in the old Third Division North, notorious as the toughest division in the Football League. Nelson, who managed to win promotion to the Second Division, may be glimpsed in action and Wigan

Two years after this, G.F.Lovell & Co Ltd of Manchester and Newport, gave away their 36 *Football Series* with their well-known 'Toffee Rex' brand. The firm had its own football team in Newport and played this in the Southern and Welsh Leagues from just after World War One until 1967, when it was disbanded. The colours of the cards are limited to white, red and grey, but they still have a very attractive quality. Some of the famous Cardiff City team are present. Amongst these are Billy Hardy, possible the best uncapped player in his day, Hugh Ferguson, who scored 282 goals in ten years with Motherwell, and Tom Farquharson, who, when he came over from Dublin in 1920, had never played soccer.

A rather unusual source of a good football set was Roche & Co Ltd of London, who gave them away in 1927 with their 'Rising Sun' Safety Paraffin matches. Their 50 *Famous Footballers*, a series of smallish (51 x 30mm) brown portraits, is quite distinctive and the selection of players is also pleasing, and goes from the well-known Alec Jackson, Bob Kelly and 'Jock' Rutherford, to long-forgotten players like A.G.Davies and H.Kemp of Notts County.

Since the earliest days of trade cards, the sweet manufacturers Barratt & Co Ltd (now with us in the form of Bassett's) has been a stalwart in the production of football cards. Not all the cards have been brilliant, but the number of different sets that the firm has produced over sixty years is impressive indeed. The variety of sets has also been great, although the *Famous Footballer* has been the backbone of the issues over the whole period.

In the 1920s, two attractive sets of Barratt caricatures were released. One, which depicts the figures on black backgrounds, consists of 100 personalities of the time and these cards, like many of the early Barratts, have had advertisements on the reverse. Some of the players, like the Cardiff City skipper Fred Keenor, and the Arsenal captain Tom Parker, could well be described as stars. Others are obscurities today, however, such as W.Brae (Ayr United), R.McDonald (Clapton Orient) and J. Murdock (Airdrieonians). The 1920s were a golden age for these humorous pictures, which certainly add something to a collection and in most cases were extremely well drawn. The other set of 12 action pictures contained notabilities like 'Dixie' Dean, Billy Hardy and Jimmy Ruffell.

One conventional, but useful Barratt set is recorded in the British Trade Index as *Cricketers, Footballers and Football Teams*. Only three cards of teams are known to have been issued, but around 200 of the black and white individual portraits must have been produced. These are somewhat reminiscent of the press photographs of the time, such as appeared in the old 'Athletic News'. Although the firm was sited in Wood Green, there was a fair coverage of Scottish football and included such players as T.Curry (Aberdeen), W.Dougal (Falkirk) and the illustrious Hugh Ferguson of Motherwell. Among the lesser lights from south of the border are Charles Petrie (Swindon Town) and Frank Vallis, the Merthyr Town goalkeeper who was born in Bristol and at one time was on the books of Bristol City.

One of the extremely original sets that have tended to distinguish Barratt & Co as producers is known as *Football Teams — 1st. Division*. Every current First Division side was represented by three cards. Four players appeared on each, so that a first-team squad could be built up. Some teams are obviously more famous than others and this becomes more acute with the passing of time. Arsenal, for instance, were just beginning to approach their peak and the cards show such stars as the legendary Alex James, whose baggy, knee-length shorts were a trademark, Herbie Roberts, the first 'policeman' centre-half, Eddie Hapgood, the great England left-back, David Jack and 'Boy' Bastin from Exeter. Most of the teams have some famous names, however. Blackpool have, for example, Jimmy Hampson, the prolific but ill-fated goalscorer from Nelson, who was drowned on a fishing trip near Fleetwood. Birmingham City have Harry Hibbs, who kept goal for them for sixteen years and Grimsby Town include the pint-sized inside-forward Jackie Bestall, one of the most famous names in the history of the club.

One further series of football interest that is worthy of mention in this chapter is the D.C. Thomson issue of 32 *Football Towns and Their Crests*, a joint promotion venture of the 'Adventure', 'Rover', 'Skipper' and 'Wizard'. Although no footballers are featured in this series, these cards are both attractive and informative. They are quite large (around 80 x 65mm and cut from pairs) and date from some time in the mid-1920s. On every card four coloured crests of football towns or cities are shown on a white background. The selection of the teams and the information on the backs, although brief, make them particularly interesting. Along with the teams we would expect to see today, we can find defunct clubs like Durham City, amateur teams like St Alban's City and such obscurities as Inverness Citadel FC. We can learn that St James' Gate wore red and played at Iveagh Park or that Durham City wore blue and gold hoops and played at Holiday Park. It is unfortunate that many cards from this period are very difficult to obtain today and have greatly increased in price in recent years.

Various odd cards and sets that are both very scarce and somewhat obscure turn up from time to time. For instance, a local Wolverhampton firm called Paulton's used to produce cards of Wanderers players at this time. The British Trade Index includes details of 36 cards which were brought out to commemorate the 1923-4 season, when the club won the Third Division North championship. These even include one card of the Board members and another of the trainer, 'Geordie' Holley. However, the firm was certainly issuing cards at a later period and around 1928 another series was released which included L.Botto, a goalkeeper from Durham City, Tom Pritchard, a centre-half signed from Newport County and Dai Richards, a Merthyr wing-half later capped for Wales.

Apart from the numerous sets we have covered from many sources, various series of mixed sporting

Athletic. Unlike the *Pinnace* cards, these have good biographical backs, where we may discover, for instance, that Tommy Cairns, the Glasgow Rangers centre-forward, had played for Bristol City and that Jimmy Carmichael, the Grimsby Town goalscorer, had previously been with Mid-Rhondda (an old Southern League outfit in Tonypandy, which went by the unlikely nickname of the 'Mushrooms'.)

As stated before, this 'Rover' series was published with anonymous backs, but various similar cards were produced with the name of the publisher on the reverse. The 'Gem', the 'Magnet' and 'Nelson Lees' were among the publications that produced such items around 1922. Although many of the players, such as A.V.Hutchins (Arsenal), Frank Reilly (Blackburn Rovers) and Alec Donaldson (Sunderland) are now just names, they must have been considerable personalities at the time. The 'Champion', which was published by the Amalgamated Press Limited, of London, issued black and white portraits of footballers and other sportsmen at the same period. Their series of *Famous Football Captains* included such worthies as Fred Parker of Clapton Orient and Reg Freeman of Oldham Athletic.

Some of the other black and white cards show more originality. D.C.Thomson's 'Adventure', for instance, put out a set of cards with autographed backs, where we can see the signatures of such personalities as Elisha Scott, the legendary goalkeeper, and Len Davies, who enjoyed an illustrious career with Cardiff City, before ending his playing days with Bangor City. In 1922, the 'Gem' produced an *Autographed Real Action Shot Series*, where one of the stars we can see is Alf Quantrill of Preston North End, the son-in-law of Steve Bloomer and later a successful insurance broker.

In 1924, the 'Rover' issued a well-produced set entitled *This Year's Top Form Footballers*. These sepia photographs on brown card show some well-respected faces of British football, including Hughie Gallacher, in a Newcastle United jersey, Jimmy Ruffell of West Ham United and West Bromwich Albion's Tommy Glidden, the most famous of the footballing brothers.

The set of 'Adventure and Vanguard Football Photos' (1925) is interesting, more for the subject matter than for the conventional black and white photographs. Some lesser-known players in the series include Harold 'Dusty' Miller (fifteen seasons with the Pensioners, but not as well remembered as many today), Robert Bennie of Airdrieonians, a Scottish FA Cup winner and international and Robert Rock, the Kilmarnock centre-forward.

Other monochrome series include the 'Adventure's' *Famous British Footballers*, a set of portraits with a broad gold surround issued by 'Vanguard', and the Champion's 22 *English League (Div 1) Footer Captains*, given away between January and April 1926. In fact, most of these periodical series would have been issued piece-meal, in order to retain the captive 'audience' for a reasonable length of time. 'Boys Magazine', a name we have already come across, produced a series of sepia sporting photographs, mainly soccer, at around this period. Despite the slightly varying size of the cards (they were apparently cut down from strips of four) and the normally blank backs, the set has definite merits. Stan Davies of West Bromwich Albion is shown wearing his international cap, a habit we no longer see, either because they have become devalued or because of a change of outlook.

Not all of the series put out of these boys' magazines were monochrome, and a particularly bright example is 'Sport and Adventure's' set of 46 *Famous Footballers* (1922). Apart from such famous stars as Charlie Buchan and Billy Meredith, we may find lesser mortals, like I.Boocock, Bradford City's left-back and the unfortunate Bullock of Huddersfield Town, who died at the age of 36 after drinking cleaning fluid. Other series of this nature that can be found include Chum's 'Real Colour Photos' and D.C.Thomson's *British Team of Footballers* (1923). The latter are hand-coloured three-quarter portraits and include Kenny Campbell, New Brighton's Scottish goalkeeper and Liverpool's 'Jock' McNabb.

Before we leave this field of periodicals behind us, it is worth mentioning the booklets that were produced at this time. These were of a high standard and were often of a superior quality to cards. In 1925 the 'Adventure' issued three booklets — *Cup Fighters of 1925, Star Footballers of 1925* and *Great Players of Today*. The colour photographs include one of Bolton Wanderers' great forward-line and a team picture of Queen's Park FC. In 1927, the same publication produced *Coloured Photos of Star Footballers*.

The 'Triumph', one of the Amalgamated Press magazines, issued a particularly important series, from the historical viewpoint, in 1924-5. The five 'Photo Albums' include blue and white team photographs of all the Football League sides (except, for some reason, Wrexham) and the Scottish First Division teams. Apart from the star sides, we can see defunct clubs, such as Aberdare Athletic, Ashington, Durham City and New Brighton, and lesser teams like Crewe Alexandra, Hartlepools United and Rochdale, that have somehow managed to survive. The Tranmere Rovers picture includes a rare shot of 'Dixie' Dean in his pre-Everton period.

Apart from these boys' magazines, various other trade firms began to produce football cards, another departure from the pre-1918 era. One of the first of these to issue a set of footballers was Lacey's Chewing Wax, with their 50 sepia *Footballers*. These rather drab photographs showed, among others, Stan Seymour (Newcastle United), Tommy Clay (the Tottenham Hotspur right-back) and the immortal Hughie Gallacher, in his early days with Airdrieonians.

In 1924, John Filshill Ltd of Glasgow issued a set of 25 *Footballers* with their 'Lotus' toffee. The firm released only three sets of cards altogether, but this one is especially attractive, having portraits in an oval, with an artistic surround. Because of the Scottish base of the firm, various players from north of the border are in the series. Amongst them are L.McMillan (Hamilton Academical), G.French and W.Rankin (Greenock Morton) and H.Ritchie of Hibernian.

South African forward who scored a record 17 hat-tricks for Liverpool, Swindon Town's Bert Denyer, the first London boy to win a schoolboy cap, and George Maddison, Hull City's long-serving goalkeeper.

One series that we must mention here, although it was actually issued in January, 1930, is John Player's set of 50 *Association Cup Winners*. Although the pictorial quality is somewhat sombre, with the dark brown backgrounds, the set is both unusual and historically important. These retrospective cards show eleven small individual pictures of Cup-winning sides, from the rise of the professionals in 1883. Although we may regret that the earlier amateurs were not included, the cards show players not covered in other sets. The short-lived Blackburn Olympic, who made the professional breakthrough, are shown with their fine half-back, John Hunter. He was born more than 130 years ago and all of his contemporaries are now strictly historical figures. Many other fine old teams and players can be seen in this series — Blackburn Rovers, with Herbie Arthur and James Forrest, the first professional to play for England; West Bromwich Albion, with Billy Bassett, 'Spry' Woodhall and Jem Bayliss; and Preston North End, in prouder days, with Ross and Goodall.

The Player's sets tend to be extremely typical of the cigarette producer, with 50 cards in standard size. The Ogden's set *Captains of A.F.Clubs and Colours*, on the other hand, had the unusual number of 44 cards, although this was clearly to cover all of the First and Second Division clubs of the time. One the fronts were well-executed colour portraits and on the backs, unusually, lists of the eleven first-team members, with their weights and heights. Among the well-known faces of the period, such as Arsenal's Charlie Buchan, we can see such lesser mortals as J.Poole (Bradford City), G.Malcolm (Darlington), W.Briscoe (Port Vale) and D.Hutchinson (South Shields).

The cards put out by the cigarette companies we have covered tend to have their own character and many are very impressive. The difference compared with the pre-1918 period lies in the fact that these were supplemented by large numbers of trade cards and in particular by those put out by boys' periodicals. At that time, as is the case today, cards were 'given' away in order to induce youngsters to purchase a particular comic or magazine. At that time these were more story papers than the picture comics of today. These periodical cards tend to follow two different patterns, the monochrome team and miniature portrait cards, all extremely similar in design, and the other, more adventurous sets that differed with the individual publication.

Various boys' papers published small black and white team photographs in the 1922-3 period and, indeed, they are so similar in format that it is necessary to look at the back of the card in order to establish exactly who produced it. 'The Magnet' (famous for Billy Bunter), 'Pluck', 'Chums', and 'Boys Magazine', were all responsible for such issues. Although there is nothing fancy about them, and the boys they were aimed at may well have preferred something a bit more colourful, from a historical point of view they certainly give a useful picture of the age and numerous less fashionable teams are to be found there.

In the 'Boys Magazine' series we can see Plymouth Argyle, with Atterbury and Moses Russell, and Edinburgh Hibernian (probably so called to distinguish them from Dundee United, then known as Dundee Hibernian.) The 'Chums' series shows a picture of the Lancashire side, Nelson, in their brief moment of glory, as well as more prominent teams like Manchester City, with their bespectacled goalkeeper J.F.Mitchell, who was an amateur and full England 'cap'. Likewise to be seen are Cardiff City, with their contemporary heroes, Joe Clennell, Billy Turnbull and Jimmy Gill. The 'Pluck' collection of sides has particular appeal. Few such sets would include a picture of Crewe Alexandra. Apart from Barnsley and Bury we can find Clapton Orient, with the former Spurs player, Bertie Bliss and the long-serving goalkeeper Arthur Wood, who made 374 Football League appearances for the 'O's. There is also a photograph of Walsall, with their player-manager Albert Groves. His brother, George, can be seen in the *Pinnace* series and the latter's son, the Welsh international Billy Lucas, stayed with Albert when a teenager with Wolverhampton Wanderers.

Less well-known than these black and white cards are the sepia inserts that were given away with the same kind of publications. Although similar in content (indeed, some of the photographs are identical), the format is much larger, more like the size of a magazine photograph, and they are therefore much easier to scrutinize. They were printed on flimsy paper and, though many can be found from the early and mid 1920s, the issue of such inserts seems to have died out by the 1930s. 'Boys Magazine' produced some fine examples over roughly a five-year period. It is no surprise to find Plymouth here once again, for the Argyle just failed to achieve promotion to the Second Division for six consecutive years in the 1920s. Cardiff City, who reached the FA Cup Final in two years out of three, are also present again and other teams include Glasgow Celtic, Glasgow Rangers and Bristol City. The 'Pals' series of 1923-4 contains, amongst others, Nelson, Crystal Palace, Bristol City and the defunct Scottish side, Third Lanark.

As well as black and white team photographs, numerous small player portraits were also given away at this time. While the team photographs tended to measure around 70 x 45mm, most of these player portraits were about 35 x 45mm, although some were produced in pairs. By far the largest series was similar in format to the *Pinnace* cards. The backs are anonymous, but apparently the cards were given away with the D.C.Thomson publication, the 'Rover'. Over a hundred issues were released and there was a distinct Scottish bias. Browsing through the cards we may glimpse such notables of the time as Billy Devlin (Clyde), who played for various clubs south of the border, Jimmy Dunn (Edinburgh Hibernians), Peter Gaffney, the Alloa Athletic centre-half and Carl Hansen (Glasgow Rangers), a Danish centre-forward from Copenhagen

Borough, whose 1930-31 mid-season demise robbed the town of League football for almost fifty years. The Scottish action cards include Clyde v Arthurlie and show Dempster, the Bo'ness goalkeeper, making a save in their first Division One game.

The group of coloured portraits includes the two most celebrated goalscorers of the 1920s, George Camsell and William Ralph 'Dixie' Dean. In the early post-war period the ratio of goals-per-match had been disappointingly low due to well-organised defensive ploys, especially in the case of Bill McCracken and his offside game. Because of this, the offside rule was changed in 1925, so that only two opponents instead of three had to be between the forward and the opposing goal. Attackers had a field-day, as defences grappled with the new situation. On the first day of the new rule Aston Villa thrashed Burnley 10-0 and large scores became commonplace. Centre-forwards achieved large tallies during the course of a season and in 1927 George Camsell of Middlesbrough hit the back of the net 59 times. The following season 'Dixie' Dean of Everton, who a few years earlier had survived an horrific motorcycle accident, unbelievably went one better. He needed a hat-trick in his last game against Arsenal and made history by achieving it. This record is unlikely to be beaten. 'Dixie' was one of a long line of goalscoring Merseyside forwards that has included, amongst others, Tommy Lawton, Dave Hickson, Roger Hunt and Ian Rush in the present era. Another interesting inclusion in this series is the sound goalkeeper Jack Hacking, one of Oldham Athletic's few internationals and the father of another professional footballer.

The brown back *Famous Footballers* are coloured portraits, with many being team captains, as is the case with Fred Kean (Sheffield Wednesday), Fred Reed (West Bromwich Albion) and Billy Birrell (Middlesbrough). Some lesser-known names today include George Harkus, the Southampton centre-half, Tom Greaves, the Darlington full-back, and Sid Binks, the Blackpool defender, who had earlier been a free scorer with the North-Eastern amateur club Bishop Auckland. Also in the series we find Sam Wynne of Oldham Athletic, who, in 1923, had the unique experience of scoring two penalties and two own-goals in a memorable match with Manchester United.

The *Footballers in Action* set probably dates, in fact, from the second half of 1927, as there are many shots of the famous 1927 FA Cup Final, in which Cardiff City defeated Arsenal by one goal to nil, to take the Cup out of England for the only time. In this particular series there are many pleasing action pictures and a shot of the rival skippers shaking hands before the kick-off. Cardiff City were determined Cup battlers, who had reached Wembley two years earlier, and Arsenal were on the threshold of their great spell. At the time of writing, Ernie Curtis of the City is still alive, as are the Gunners Joe Hulme and Tom Parker. The game was ironically decided when Arsenal's Welsh goalkeeper, Dan Lewis, let the ball slip through his hands. To this day the side has retained a ritual of washing new goalkeepers' jerseys, as the ball was considered to have slipped into the net off the lanolin. Lewis himself was a very keen sportsman, and playing bowls when he died.

Another intriguing card shows the well-known goalkeeper Howard Baker in action for the Corinthians in an FA Cup tie against Newcastle United. Because of their amateur principles the Corinthians steered clear of the FA Cup for many years, but finally decided to enter. The team, which never had its own ground, eventually merged with Casuals, as their star began to wane. In their heyday, however, they were an institution and had a standing all their own.

John Player & Son, of Nottingham, could claim, along with W.D.&H.O.Wills, to be the foremost of cigarette card producers and obviously amongst their cards are series of football interest. These are of this manufacturer's usual high standard. Several sets were put out in the mid 1920s and two of these are unlike pre-1918 issues in consisting of caricatures. The earlier cards had tended to demonstrate a more sober and serious approach, but the caricatures of 'Rip' and 'Mac', possibly because they were a product of the 'Gay Twenties', show a playful and light-hearted touch. The oft-seen 'Rip' cartoons, issued in 1926, are attractively drawn and also benefit from well-researched biographical backs. Half of the players are drawn from Rugby Union, but here are numerous pictures of such prominent soccer players as Frank Barson (Manchester United), Frank Roberts (Manchester City) and Norman Bullock, a leading centre-half with Bury at a time when they were a more illustrious team than they are today.

The 'Rip' set consists of 50 cards, as does the 'Mac' issue, which was produced the following year. The set is of much the same high standard and consists of coloured caricatures on a pale orange background, the reverses having informative texts. There are thirteen Rugby Union personalities in the series, but the rest are soccer players, from a great variety of clubs. It is not just the big city sides that are represented. Present are such notables of the time as Bury's winger Wally Amos, Fulham's brave goalkeeper Ernie Beecham, whose career was blighted by injury, and Plymouth Argyle's Cornish centre-forward, Jack Cock, who had won the Military Medal in World War One. A couple of prominent amateurs are also included — Millwall's Ghent-born centre-half, W.I.Bryant and Lieutenant K.E.Hegan of The Army and Corinthians, who later reached the rank of Lieutenant-Colonel and won the OBE. Both were full internationals for England. The role of the amateur decreased with the years and Bernard Joy in the 1930s was the last to wear the full England shirt, although George Robb in 1954 won a cap not long after turning professional. Nowadays, of course, it would be unthinkable for an amateur to play for the full England side.

In 1928, John Player & Son produced a set entitled, not unreasonably, *Footballers of 1928*, followed a short time later by a supplementary set of 25. Some rugby players are included in this series of coloured action drawings and amongst the soccer pictures are such stars as Gordon Hodgson, the interest were issued at this period, such as 36 *Sporting Celebrities in Action*, produced by Major Drapkin & Co of London. These photographic cards were issued overseas, mainly in Australia and New Zealand, and include Jimmy McMullan and David Jack.

The sets and manufacturers covered in this chapter illustrate the depth and variety of coverage that was devoted to soccer at this time. It was the national winter game, and the cards and other material concerned with the game reflect the degree of public interest in professional football. The amateur side of soccer is also covered, but in the main we see only a handful of talented players who managed to hold their own in the professional game. Amateur football was now second-class and largely restricted to people playing for their own enjoyment, in their spare time.

One aspect of football that is noticeably absent from cards at this period is coverage of the foreign game. The Home Championship dominated British soccer and an insular attitude blotted out the abilities of foreign sides, even though British teams had often played against them and individual players had appeared for British clubs.

Player's 'Association Cup Winners' issued in the late 1920s.

Pattrieoux 'photographic' cards (1920s).

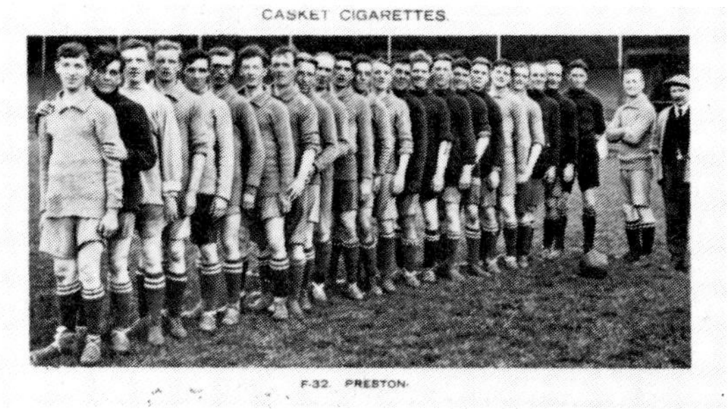

Boys magazines 1920.

B.BATEMAN

S.TONNER

F.WALDEN

A.M.DUCAT

H.BAGGE

A.A.DOMINY

D.MERCER

D.J.COCK

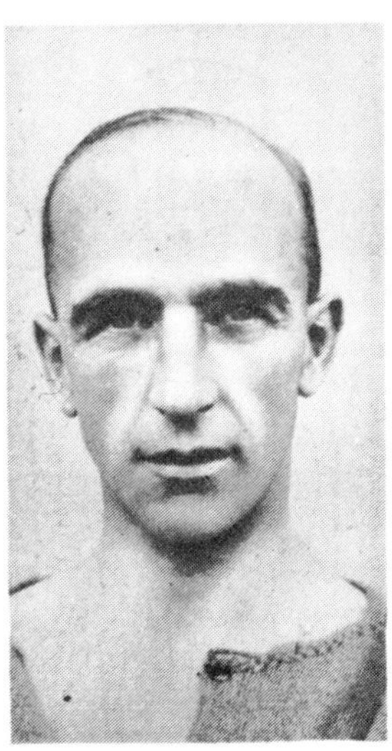

J.A.CROAL

D.H.SHEA

T.G.BROMILOW

T.F.HODDINOTT

Hill's 'Famous Footballers' 1923.

Boys magazine items 1920s.

Top: Pinnace. Bottom: Barratt's 'Football Teams', c1928.

Various 1920s issues.

Rare Wolves, late 1920s.

The Arsenal Years
The 1930s to World War Two

TO make a distinction between the 1920s and the 1930s is to a great extent artificial, but somewhere around the turn of the decade the old era began to peter out and the roots of modern football began. Perhaps this may best be illustrated by looking at two of the longest serving and most famous players in the history of the game, both, by chance, wingers. Billy Meredith, the Welsh Wizard, had commenced his career in the 1890s, not long after the foundation of the Football League. After World War One he resumed his career, like many other veterans of the period, and still had enough ability to play in Manchester City's first team in the early 1920s. Stanley Matthews, now Sir Stanley, started as an amateur with Stoke City in September 1930 and, after a monumental career, in which his name became a household word, he was playing in a second spell for Stoke City as late as 1965.

Some time around 1930 there was a change of outlook in professional football. Although there was still plenty of amateurism in boardrooms, there was an increasing professionalism in playing matters. The old secretary-manager was gradually being replaced by the new professional manager. The most significant figure in this field was Herbert Chapman, the 'Football Emperor'. Although never an outstanding player himself, Chapman had an outstanding feel for football management. Having taken the obscure and fairly recently formed Huddersfield Town to three consecutive League Championships, he turned his talents to Highbury and made Arsenal the best known name in world football. It is really with the rise of Arsenal that the modern era begins.

Since, as stated earlier, the distinction drawn between the two decades is largely artificial, there is clearly little difference in the overall pattern of card production. The issue of standard sets of cigarette cards at this time, however, was particularly impressive and series such as the two Wills' sets of *Association Footballers* are archetypes of the popular conception of the cigarette card.

One of the first football sets to be released in the 1930s was, indeed, a particularly fine series of 50 *Footballers* (1930-31), issued by the London firm of Lambert and Butler in January 1931. These attractively drawn colour portraits of stars of the day showed, among others, Eric Brook, Len Davies and the 'Wembley Wizard', Alan Morton.

Two years later another impressive and quite individual series was issued, 50 *A.F.C. Nicknames*. Two firms gave the set away with their cigarettes, Ogden's Ltd and Hignett Bros & Co, the difference being that today the Hignett cards are more expensive due to their greater scarcity. The fronts show coloured cartoons based on the nicknames of the clubs, so that Wolverhampton Wanderers are represented by a wolf and Northampton Town by a cobbler. The attraction is in the pictorial design. The cartoons are especially well drawn and the backgrounds are made out of the club colours, which adds to the visual impact. The reverses give a resumé of the individual club's history.

An innovation of the 1930s was the introduction of 'stickybacks'. The adhesive backs were intended for the cards to be stuck down in specially produced albums. Many of the cards were collected loose, however, and these are considerably more valuable than cards stuck in albums. Serious collectors have tended to look down on these adhesive sets, but overall they were well produced, because of the large number of cards given away. One of the great dangers for the unsuspecting collector, however, is that, if not treated with the greatest caution, the cards have a nasty habit of congealing into a useless, valueless mess. The frustration is indescribable.

One of the first of these adhesive sets dealing with football was issued by the London firm Ardath Tobacco Co Ltd in October 1934 and was entitled 50 *Famous Footballers*. Some of the stars depicted include Willis Edwards, the Leeds United captain, Tom Graham, connected with Nottingham Forest for over fifty years, and Alf Strange, the Sheffield Wednesday international who later became a poultry farmer.

Two other adhesive sets produced at this period were issued by Stephen Mitchell and Son of Glasgow with their 'Prize Crop' cigarettes. Although the brown photographs are a little monotonous, what gives them more interest is the fact that both series are restricted to Scottish players alone. Just about all the Scottish League sides seem to be covered and it is refreshing to see some of the more obscure players of the time rather than the same old faces. *Scottish Footballers* (issued in 1934) consists of 50 portraits and alongside better known players, such as the record goalscorer Jimmy McGrory and Matt Armstrong, of Aberdeen fame, we can see the likes of Jacky Gardiner, the Queen's Park right-half.

Scottish Football Snaps, of 1935, contains 50 action photographs. George Brown, the captain of Glasgow Rangers' 1935 Scottish Cup winning side, is shown shaking hands with King George V. It was a rare event for Hamilton Academical to reach the Cup Final, and their captain, J. Bulloch, can be seen in the series, as well as their winger, J. King. Other lesser known performers of the day include the wingers John McPhee (Albion Rovers) and Andy McCall (Ayr United) and the St Johnstone centre-half, Frank Moulds.

The London firm of Carreras Ltd produced three sets of football interest in the 1930s, all of which are quite attractive and relatively cheap, as cigarette cards go. The 75 *Footballers*, issued in August, 1934, are tastefully drawn and among the personalities that can be seen are the Burnley goalkeeper, Tom Hetherington, the Blackburn Rovers' ball artist, Jack Bruton, and Maurice Webster, the Middlesbrough centre-half who started with Stalybridge Celtic.

In January 1936, a set of 48 *Popular Footballers* was issued. Some interesting characters are to be found there. Joe Kennaway, the Glasgow Celtic goalkeeper, was an international for Scotland, Canada and the United States, and George Stephenson (Charlton Athletic), the brother of Clem, had started with the wound-up Leeds City. The biographical details on Tudor Martin are inaccurate. Although stated to be a Swansea Town local discovery, he, in fact, commenced his career with West Bromwich Albion and then joined Newport County, where he still holds the club record of 34 goals in a season. Some players from smaller clubs are to be found on the cards and amongst these are Eric Hayward, the Port Vale centre-half, and Albert Turner, who helped Doncaster Rovers to promotion.

Slightly earlier, in September 1935, Carreras issued 48 *Famous Footballers*, but the second 24 were later redrawn and re-issued. The players included in the series are mainly stars, such as George Camsell, Stanley Matthews and Hughie Gallacher. Lesser-known players can be found and among these is J.C.Burns, Brentford's amateur international left-half.

The Manchester company of J.A.Pattreiouex, mentioned previously as benefactors of the football collector, in 1934 brought out a photographic set of 78 *Footballers in Action*, inserted in their 'Senior Service', 'Trawler' and 'Illingworth' packets. Why this strange number of cards should have been selected is difficult to understand. Among the black and white cards can be seen Jim Allen, Portsmouth's stopper centre-half, Tom Gardner, Aston Villa's long-throw expert, and Frank Moss, the Arsenal goalkeeper, who retired through injury in 1936.

R. & J.Hill Ltd produced two very collectable sets of cards in this pre-war period. In 1935 came 50 *Popular Footballers*, these black and white photographs really making up two sets. Series A was numbered 1-30 and Series B 31-50, the first being more expensive today because of greater scarcity. There was a West Country bias to this set which is most unusual. Apart from stars like the Welsh international forward 'Pat' Glover and the Irish goalscorer Joe Bambrick, one can see players like G.H.Stabb (Torquay United), a 'village green discovery', and his team-mates John Jones and Tom Pickersgill.

In 1939 the Company produced 50 *Famous Footballers* and, shortly afterwards, a supplementary set of 25 appeared, numbered 51-75. These squat-looking cards have very colourful portraits and a pleasing blend of players, which does not ignore the smaller clubs. In the series are such players as Billy Hullett (Plymouth Argyle), a well-known performer after the war with Merthyr Tydfil, John Shadwell, the Exeter City right-half, Reading's Dennis Watkin, who also played cricket for Nottinghamshire, and L.G.Sullivan, the Chesterfield left winger. Also shown is Alec Herd, who in 1951 appeared in the same Stockport County side as his son, David, both playing at inside-forward.

Apart from the excellent *A.F.C. Nicknames*, which has already been mentioned, two other football series were also issued by the Liverpool firms of Ogden's and Hignett. One was 50 *Football Caricatures*, which came out in September 1935, and these colourful and attractively drawn cards have very good biographies on the backs. The caricatures were executed by the redoubtable 'Mac' and are full of movement. The stars depicted include Cliff Britton, an Everton player and later manager, Cuthbert 'Charlie' Phillips, Wolverhampton Wanderers' Welsh international winger, and Alex Massie, the well-known Scottish performer bought by Aston Villa. Some Rugby League players are also present, including the famous Stan Brogden of Leeds.

In the same year 50 *Football Club Captains* appeared. These bright stickybacks show not only soccer players, but many Rugby League performers, amongst them the immortal Jim Sullivan, who some years ago had a street named after him. All of the First Division club captains are present in the series, including such well-known personalities as the Welsh international captain Tom Griffiths (Middlesbrough), Arthur Rowe, later manager of the 'push and run' Tottenham Hotspur side, and Dan Blair (Aston Villa), who, like quite a few other players of the period, had begun his career in North America. With many of the sets of this era the colour quality is far superior to that seen in earlier years and more lifelike.

A firm which produced three modest but very welcome sets in the 1930s was John Sinclair Ltd of Newcastle-on-Tyne. The first was a fairly conventional series of monochrome portrait and action photographs, entitled *English and Scottish Football Stars*. Despite the title, not all could be described as stars, although they were undoubtedly good players. An interesting card shows Bob Kelly in his later Carlisle United days, well towards the end of his career. Some other personalities to be seen include Bert Trentham, an FA Cup winner with West Bromwich Albion, Jack Coulter, Everton's Irish winger, and Mark Hooper, the Sheffield Wednesday forward who started as a goalkeeper.

The other two sets, although quite unpretentious in their concept, are quite unusual and are a welcome addition to any collection. The 50 *Well-known Footballers* (North-Eastern Counties) and *Well-known Footballers* (Scottish), both issued in 1938, are in the same style and show photographic heads on caricature bodies. The result, on a plain white background, is very attractive. The North-Eastern cards are especially welcome because of the unusual concentration on that 'hotbed of soccer'. Naturally enough the set mainly concerns the big three, Newcastle United, Sunderland and Middlesbrough. Also included, however, are representatives of the smaller clubs, Darlington, Hartlepools United and the unlucky Gateshead, who lost their League position to Peterborough in 1960.

With the three big clubs, virtually the first-team squad is shown. The Sunderland team at this time was particularly impressive, beating Preston North End 3-1 in the 1937 FA Cup Final. Raich Carter was a great player, who dominated the football scene before and after World War Two, and even founded his own magazine, the 'Soccer Star'. The long-serving Mapson is also in the set, as are Sunderland's three talented wingers of the time, Len Duns, Eddie Burbanks and Jimmy Connor. The Middlesbrough side includes the able forwards George Camsell (then in the veteran stage), Mickey Fenton, Ralph Birkett and Benny Yorston.

The players representing the smaller North-Eastern teams are, in general, more obscure, such as Albert Harris (Darlington), a winger who had been with Newcastle United and Barnsley. Albert McInroy is shown with Gateshead, however, and in a Hartlepools United shirt is the centre-half David Davidson, who had gained a Cup winners' medal with Newcastle United in 1932, two years after his transfer there for £4,500.

The Scottish set used the same formula just as successfully. Some of the players were quite famous and others considerably less so. Ben Ellis was a Welshman who somehow ended up as Motherwell's left-back, and the Scot Jimmy Delaney (Glasgow Celtic) equalled a record by obtaining Scottish, English and Irish Cup winners' medals with Celtic, Manchester United and Derry City. It is pleasing to see players from the smaller Scottish clubs and these include Ken Dawson, the Falkirk left winger, Bobby Rennie, the Dundee full-back and the Arbroath centre-half Charlie Gavin.

The two Wills series are, as stated previously, the quintessence of the cigarette card. These colourful stickybacks were printed in great numbers and are well remembered by former boy collectors, not least since they came right at the end of cigarette card production. The first series of 50 *Association Footballers*, described in the catalogues as 'with frameline', was released in November 1935. They were classic colour portraits, with good biographies on the reverse. Pre-war football must have been at its peak at this period, before its slide into wartime slump. Two examples of the personalities shown are Ted Sandford (West Bromwich Albion), the nephew of Abe Jones, an old Albion player, and John McMenemy, the son of the old Glasgow Celtic performer, James McMenemy.

The second series of 50 *Association Footballers* (no frameline), which was apparently released in November 1939, follows the same formula as the first. The beginning of hostilities was marked by the so-called 'phoney war' and this series must have appeared in the lull before the war brought an end to cigarette card production, as we know it. This set has a pleasing mixture of major and minor teams, and alongside the stars we can see such players as Gilbert Alsop (Walsall), who found fame when his team knocked mighty Arsenal out of the FA Cup, Norman Low, now living in Canada, who led Newport County to an unexpected promotion in 1939, and Tommy Bamford, a Welsh international with Wrexham. In the old peacock colours of Leeds United can be seen Eric Stephenson, who was not to survive the war.

Some sets are much dearer and more difficult to obtain than others, but this does not necessarily mean that they are in any way superior. A case in point is the set of 50 *Popular Footballers* produced by United Services Manufacturing Co Ltd of London in 1936. These cards have always been fairly expensive, presumably due to limited production. Although the format is similar to that used in R. & J.Hill's *Famous Footballers* three years later, the United Services' cards are not coloured, but brown and white and the effect is fairly drab. The usual run of players is present, eg. Raich Carter, Herbie Roberts and Eddie Hapgood.

Three almost identical series were produced by the firm of Godfrey Phillips Ltd and in mint condition these cards are as attractive as any to be found, with their bright colours and overall production quality. The three sets of 50 were *International Caps* and *Famous Footballers*, issued in 1936 and *Soccer Stars*, which came out the following year. The picture format is the same and many of the same players turn up in all three sets, the only difference being in the backs. Quite a few Welsh players are to be found in these series, such as Eugene 'Taffy' O'Callaghan (Leicester City), Bob John (Arsenal) and the great Fred Keenor, shown at the end of his career, with Tunbridge Wells Rangers.

The two W.A. & A.C.Churchman series of 50 *Association Footballers*, released in September 1938 and September 1939, have been criticised because, as with a number of Churchman sets at this time, they were restricted to brown and white. By and large these action shots are quite effective, however, and the overall impact is rather more pleasing than is the case with the United Services cards.

Many players from this period re-appeared after the war and men like Len Goulden, 'Sandy' McNab and Vic Woodley resumed their careers in 1945, however briefly. The 1938-9 season was Ipswich Town's first in League football and, since the firm was situated in that town, Bill Dale and the goalkeeper Mickey Burns are to be found on the cards.

Amongst the personalities chosen to appear in the second set, prepared for the ill-starred 1939-40 season, are Bernard Joy, the last amateur to play for England, Tom Brolly, Millwall's Irish international, Freddie Steele (Stoke City) and Beaumont Asquith, Manchester United's centre-forward. A young Wilf Mannion can be seen and he was destined to become one of the greats of the immediate post-war period.

For the football historian possibly the most important of the cigarette card producers in the 1930s was Ardath Tobacco Co Ltd, a London firm. Apart from the conventional series of 50 *Famous Footballers*, which is fairly run of the mill, the company also created many photographic sets. While at the time of issue these black and white cards may have had less appeal than the numerous coloured ones around, the Ardath productions give a good overall view of the football scene. Between 1937 and 1939 Ardath released numerous series of general interest — various sportsmen, cinema stars and so forth. What is of much more direct interest, however, is the series of football team cards produced in the 1936-7 period. Six series, lettered A to F, were issued, each dealing with a specific geographical region and these were followed by a supplementary squarer issue (76 x 60mm), entitled *Album of Great Players*, was given away. This had a blue album and again English and Scottish versions were produced.

In the series of miniature *Panel Portraits* are players such as the Grimsby Town goalkeeper George Tweedy, who started his career as a centre-forward, Billy Bagley, Portsmouth's reserve in the 1939 FA Cup Final, Jimmy Hagan in his early Derby County days and Torry Gillick, who had cost Everton £8,000 when signed from Glasgow Rangers. In the English version of *Stars of Today* we can see Joe James, Brentford's six-foot centre-half, Arsenal's Alf Kitchen and Bill Bryant, Manchester United's winger from Wrexham. Also present is the ubiquitous Charlie Fletcher. First seen with the defunct Merthyr Town he was now with Ipswich Town in their first season in League football. In the Scottish series are to be found the likes of George Robertson (Kilmarnock), Alex Sharp (Falkirk) and John Kirk of Clyde.

The *Album of Great Players* is another worthwhile series, although how great the players are is open to question. Even the players with top clubs are not all well-remembered today. Tottenham Hotspur had an outside right by the name of Fred Sergeant and Arsenal's Les Jones from Aberdare, although a Welsh international, was not one of their pre-war greats. One interesting face is that of Bill Shankly. His post-war exploits as a manager have tended to obscure his own fine playing record with Preston North End.

The Scottish players would certainly be struggling to be called 'great' and one of the more interesting inclusions is Mustapha Mansour, Queen's Park's signing from the Egyptian Civil Service. Other so-called greats include Andy Adams, the Arbroath right-half and John Watters, the Cowdenbeath outside-right who was previously with New Brighton.

One interesting issue was of eight very large blocks of three individual photographs, similar to the large *Panel Portraits*. One noticeable inclusion is Walter Winterbottom (Manchester United), who after the war became England's first team manager. Some of the players seen on the cards of this period are pretty obscure, but this may be explained in many cases by World War Two. Youngsters who were just making a name for themselves in the immediate pre-war period were seven years older by the time that League football returned. Many of those who did make an effort to resume their careers soon quit and a large number of others simply settled for jobs outside the game. Some of the players who can be glimpsed on these triple cards include Bill Cobley (Aston Villa), Adolf Hanson (Liverpool) and Leslie Miller of Tottenham Hotspur.

A series of eight large colour portraits was issued by the 'Topical Times' in 1936 and amongst others to be seen were Fred Tilson (Manchester City), Ken Willingham, the Huddersfield Town and England wing-half and Berry Nieuwenhuys, Liverpool's famous South African. This was not one of the publication's better issues, however.

Apart from cards the 'Topical Times' produced various other items. Indeed, boys' periodicals have always shown a great deal of imagination in the range of football ware they have produced in order to boost their readership. Around 1930 the 'Topical Times' brought out a four-part *Album of 100 Football Stars*, with colour portraits not unlike the 1935 Wills' series and with accompanying biographies. Included are a young 'Dally' Duncan in Hull City's colours and Joe Edelston, the Swindon Town outside-right. Some of the less exalted performers include W.H.Scott, the Bournemouth inside-right and D. Wilson, the Hamilton Academical centre-forward.

In 1934 the 'Topical Times' brought out a *Star Teams Photo Album*. This consisted of 32 team photographs, with an exceedingly brief history of each side. The photographs make the booklet worth collecting, and apart from the top English sides, Glasgow Celtic, Heart of Midlothian and Glasgow Rangers are also present.

The D.C.Thomson string of titles, such as the 'Adventure', 'Hotspur' and the 'Wizard', was very popular with boys for decades. One of their less impressive, but still collectable series was brought out in 1934. This was a collection of *Football Team Cards*, little coloured action pictures to illustrate the club's colours. Although there should be 64, two appear not to have been issued. Those that were released included Brighton & Hove Albion, Swindon Town, Motherwell, Gateshead, Crewe Alexandra and Southport.

Various odd items were produced for boys' magazines. The 'Adventure', for instance, created a set of six teams printed on metal — Everton, Arsenal, Sheffield Wednesday, West Bromwich Albion, Glasgow Celtic and Rangers. Metal pictures of individual players were also produced. A curious set of cards was issued by the 'Adventure', entitled *Play the Sport*. The backs were printed for a game, but the fronts were excellent miniature black and white photographs and they are well worth collecting for this reason. Some well-known performers are there, such as Matt Busby and Ted Drake, but many are unlikely to be seen elsewhere. These include Eric Oakton, Chelsea's 1932 signing from Bristol Rovers, A.Lumberg (Brighton & Hove Albion), K.Smalley (Oldham Athletic) and S.Sweetman (Millwall).

For 1934-5 the 'Champion' produced a set of football albums similar to those issued by the 'Triumph' in 1924-5, but somewhat larger in format. These blue and white photographs are, like the earlier series, immensely useful, since they provide a visual record of most of the players engaged in Football League games at the time. Two of the famous old names that can be seen as managers are David Jack with Southend United (then playing at the Kursaal) and Ted Vizard with Swindon Town. Another item of more curiosity value than anything else is the same publication's *Album of Famous Players*, which consists of pictures of star players with their autographs stuck in.

One final issue worth mentioning in connection with periodicals is the *Pilot's Album of Football Fame*. These are somewhat crude action pictures, but some very famous names are included, such as Eddie Hapgood, Stanley Matthews and Raich Carter.

ever since. The numbers in these early sets differ enormously. In the first series (1935-6) 100 cards were issued and possibly the same the following year, although the fact that these cards are unnumbered makes it difficult to establish the fact. In 1937-8 110 cards were produced, the following year 20 and in 1939-40, 110 again.

The first series consisted of black and white photographs and the following sets of sepia and white. The photographs were good, as were the biographies on the reverses. Some Rugby Union players were included, noticeably the All Blacks, but the preponderance is of soccer players. Many performers were retained for the following year's set and the picture remained the same, although there was normally some small alteration in the back, if only in the number.

Some interesting personalities are to be found among these *Famous Footballers.* Elisha Scott and R.Fulton, both with Belfast Celtic, are there, as is the still-surviving Albert Geldard, who made his Football League debut at the record young age of 15 years 156 days in 1929. Some well-known players are shown in the autumn of their careers with smaller clubs. These include Joe Bambrick (Walsall), Harry Duggan (Newport County) and Fred Tilson (Northampton Town).

A well-produced set not often seen is the 50 *Footballers* of Val 'Footer' Gum. These fairly large (70 x 59mm), squarish cards have blank backs. The photographs look original, however, and are of quite good quality. Produced in 1935, they show a mixture of portrait and action shots. Along with such players as Stanley Matthews and Stan Cullis can be seen such less exalted players as Blackpool's Irishman, Sam Jones, Blackburn Rovers' Bill Hough and Charlie Fletcher of Plymouth Argyle, whom we have seen ten years earlier in the *Pinnace* collection.

An unexpected source of football cards (using the term loosely) is Sherman's Football Pools. Two series of large pictures were issued in the late 1930s, one of teams and the other of individual players. Their series *Search-light on Famous Players* consisted of sepia portraits, sized 140 x 101mm, and many of the players really were stars, including Cliff Bastin, George Camsell, 'Dixie' Dean, Stan Cullis and the joint cricket and football international Johnny Arnold. These cards were probably issued over a fair period and the *Search-light on Famous Teams* appears to cover both the 1937-8 and 1938-9 seasons. These pictures seem to be coloured versions of black and white originals, but they are quite pleasant cards and include some interesting teams. The Irish and Welsh international sides are shown, which is something of a rarity. The two Third Division promotion 'dark horses', Tranmere Rovers and Newport County are shown, as are East Fife, who created a considerable upset by winning the 1938 Scottish FA Cup as a Second Division side, and their victims Kilmarnock.

With trade cards many items turn up from time to time that are seldom seen or are unrecorded. One rare set, for instance, was issued with Wayfarer raincoats. These very large black and white photographs were of sporting scenes, mainly soccer and cricket. There is, for example, one photograph of Jackie Bestall leading out the Grimsby Town side and another of an incident in a Newcastle United v Tottenham Hotspur match.

Boys' periodicals again produced many cards, the D.C.Thomson organisation issuing many and the 'Topical Times' being prominent in creating football series of high quality. Many of the latter's issues, such as the renowned *Panel Portraits*, are outsize as far as cards go and this may be the reason why they have been less collected than some other series. In the past it has been difficult to obtain information on these cards. At one time the only source was the 'Cigarette Card News' of 1953, but to some extent the situation has been rectified with the new Part Three of the British Trade Index. The large size of many of the items enhances the picture quality and makes them well worth acquiring.

A large number of cards was produced in the *Panel Portrait* series and this presents something of a maze to the novice collector. Most of them were given away with editions of the magazine, but some could be bought. Basic series were issued apparently annually from 1932 onwards and these tended to contain around fourteen cards, the best known being the coloured issue of 1936. Many odd cards were also produced and there were separate sets for Scotland and Ireland.

These *Panel Portraits* had a style and quality all their own, catching the atmosphere of the time. The real photographs show players, almost all with their arms crossed like some secret society, standing on muddy pitches in their old heavy boots. 'Patsy' Gallacher of Sunderland is shown against a sheet of corrugated iron and wearing a pair of creased shorts. 'Pongo' Waring (Aston Villa) is seen wearing a dirty bandage around his right knee that looks more likely to cause infection than prevent it. The players exhibit considerably less concern with sartorial elegance than many of their successors.

Many of the performers are well-known and quite a lot, like Wilf Mannion and Dennis Westcott, played on after the war. The hand-coloured series of 1936 shows classic portraits of personalities like Harry Betmead (Grimsby Town), Ephraim 'Jock' Dodds (Sheffield United) and Bert Sproston in the blue and gold of Leeds United. The Scottish cards portray, amongst others, Hutton Bremner (Motherwell), Tom Mooney (Airdrieonians) and George Thomson in the old black and gold strip of Aberdeen. Among the Irish can be found such relative obscurities as H.C.Hewitt (Linfield), wearing his international cap, Norman McCaw (Cliftonville) and John Priestley of Coleraine, who later spent eight years with Chelsea. For some reason the Irish are shown with their arms behind their backs.

Several sets of miniature *Panel Portraits* were issued. These are much smaller, but still significantly larger than the average cigarette card. They are again good quality photographs and include some interesting players from a variety of clubs. The 1937 series of miniature *Panel Portraits* was distributed to be collected in a red album. In 1938 *Stars of Today* was issued to be collected in a yellow album, with a different set being produced in Scotland. In 1936 a set of eleven cards. Unfortunately, because of the regional organisation of the sets, not every Football League club was covered. Teams in the West Country and Wales, for instance, were totally ignored. For the record, the sets were arranged as follows: A — Lancashire; B — North-Eastern counties; C — Yorkshire; D — Scotland; E — Midlands and F — London and Southern counties.

These fine black and white team photgraphs cover not only soccer but also Rugby League and Union, and not just the Football and Scottish Leagues, but all sorts of minor Leagues. We can see not only Arsenal and Chelsea, but Brunswick Methodists and Sutton United, Hednesford Town and Horwich Railway Mechanics' Institute, South Liverpool and Bacup Borough. The team members are all named on the backs, which is a decided advantage, although errors are known to exist and one or two individuals are represented by dashes.

In the Scottish series we can see the three defunct Edinburgh clubs, St Bernard's, Leith Athletic and Edinburgh City, as well as the old Stirling side, King's Park. These little teams, with their loyal bands of supporters, were not to last long after the issue of the photographs. Edinburgh City had attempted to emulate Queen's Park as an amateur side, but had a very brief and unsuccessful existence. St Bernard's, named after St Bernard's Well, an Edinburgh tourist attraction, had a much longer history and even won the Scottish FA Cup in 1895, but had fallen on hard times. Despite the brave efforts of Leith Athletic, none of these teams really survived the war.

These Ardath sets give a very clear picture of the football world in the 1930s and it is a pity that the cost of these cards has risen in recent years. The heroes of the First Division sides, the artisans of the Third Division teams, the fun players of the little amateur clubs are all there to be seen. Some well-known old players can also be found in their later managerial careers, such as Andy Wilson (with Walsall), Jack Hacking (Accrington Stanley) and Tommy Lowes (Barrow).

A series that cannot really be counted as a cigarette card issue, but was produced by a cigarette firm, was printed on the packages of Godfrey Phillips' BDV cigarettes, apparently to be used in various competitions and gift schemes. These package design footballers and sportsmen had an unusual look with their orange, black and white colours. Stars such as Matt Busby (now Sir Matt), Sam Cowan and 'Dixie' Dean were to be found amongst the illustrations. This technique seems to have been unique to the BDV set at this period, although it was used again after the war.

It is a mistake to think that cigarette cards were restricted purely to Britain and British football. Between 1930 and 1933, for instance, three sets were issued by the Vittoria Egyptian Cigarette Co of Rotterdam. A set of black and white photographs of the 1930-31 season was issued, with sides such as Eindhoven, Forward (Groningen) and Zandvoort. Coloured full-length portraits make up another series, with players like J.Dommering (Vitesse), F.Huizinga (Hilversum) and W. van Tuyl (Eindhoven) and a set of match action pictures of the 1933 season was also produced.

The number of firms issuing trade cards at this time was considerably less than those producing cigarette cards, certainly as far as football is concerned. One quite modest series well worthy of consideration is 100 *All Sports* produced by the biscuit firm de Beukelaer in 1932. This has been a relatively easy series to acquire and the small (70 x 49mm) brown and white portraits are unpretentious, but nonetheless worthwhile. The 100 cards really divide into two series of 50, one restricted to footballers and the other dealing with all other sports. The only drawback is that no team captions are given, but most are well-known players, such as Alex James, Cliff Bastin and W.G. 'Ginger' Richardson.

The name of Barratt & Co once again figures prominently amongst the trade card issuers. Although the format of their 1930s issues is completely different to that of their earlier productions, the contribution made was just as significant and the quality just as high. It is surprising, in fact, to see their set of 50 *FA Cup Winners*, issued in 1935. The set is very much based on the earlier John Player issue, although the cards are larger (70 x 53mm) and the individual photographs more spaced out. The real Barratt contribution at this time lies in their sets of team folders and in their succession of *Famous Footballers*.

For three seasons from 1932 Barratt & Co brought out Football Team folders for all First and Second Division sides. These consisted of twelve black and white individual photographs of each team, with a brief resumé of the club's history on the reverse. Unfortunately, as the name suggested, the card was designed to be folded over, but mercifully many escaped this fate. The photographs are good and the overall impact pleasing. As teams were promoted and relegated, the make-up of the sets changed. Some sides feature only once, while others are present three times, often with very little change in personnel. Folders were also issued for Scottish League teams and at least one is known to have been produced for a Third Division club (Newport County).

Many of the First Division clubs in the series had very fine sides. Arsenal are shown with their usual galaxy of stars, Manchester City with Matt Busby, Sam Cowan and Fred Tilson, Everton with 'Dixie' Dean, the long-serving Ted Sagar and their Welsh captain, Ben Williams. Some of the sides are much more obscure to us today. In the Grimsby Town team, for instance, we can see Jim Dyson, a 5ft 7in forward, Matt Moralee, who played only 27 times for the club before joining Aston Villa, and Hugh Jacobsen, who had been bought from Blyth Spartans for £20. Among the Notts County players we can find the likes of Eddie Lawrence, a Welsh international signed from Clapton Orient for £275, and George Stimpson, a right back signed from Kimberley Amateurs. Albion Rovers and St Johnstone are amongst the Scottish sides that can be seen.

Five series of *Famous Footballers* were issued in the 1930s and this successful pattern has been used

We have already mentioned the numerous sets of football cards that were produced in the 1930s, but there were quite a few series of mixed sporting interest issued and the odd footballer can be spotted in other sets. For instance, in the Wills' series *The Reign of H.M.King George V* (April 1935), No. 27 shows a picture of the Royal Box at the Cardiff City v Arsenal FA Cup Final.

In 1935 Pattreiouex produced 96 *Sporting Events and Stars* and on the cards can be seen the Manchester United team, Peter Doherty and George Eastham Senior. Godfrey Phillips' 54 *In the Public Eye* (1935) includes Hughie Gallacher and Ogden's *Champions of 1936*, a series of attractive coloured cards, includes the First Division champions, Arsenal and FA Cup winners, Sunderland. Gallaher's *Sporting Personalities* (1936) includes 'Dixie' Dean, Cliff Bastin, Harry Hibbs, Ronnie Starling, Alex James and Arsenal's George Allison, one of radio's first sports commentators.

Ardath's A Series of 50 *Sports Champions* (1935) includes six players in exactly the same format as their *Famous Footballers*. The colour portraits of R. & J.Hill's 50 *Celebrities of Sport* (1939) depict Stan Cullis, Bryn Jones, who was the record pre-war signing, Stanley Matthews and Vic Woodley, along with a host of world-famous stars, such as Fred Perry, Joe Davis, Tommy Farr and Henry Cotton.

One series that does not fall into any of the categories that have been discussed in this chapter, but must be mentioned, is the issue of Huddersfield Town footballers, apparently produced by the club. These black and white cards show photographic heads on cartoon bodies. All of the first team squad are portrayed, including Len Butt, Alf Young, Fred Goodall and Ken Willingham and even the assistant manager and secretary.

In 1939 cigarette card production was at a real peak and it is sad that it did not even gradually peter out, but was virtually destroyed overnight. The place of the cigarette firm was to be taken over by other manufacturers, but this year saw the end of an era. The players left in dribs and drabs, not all off to the trenches, as in 1914, but some to reserved occupations, others to the Fire Service and so on. From the football viewpoint, the next seven years were to be wasted in terms of careers and many players were never to realise their true potential.

JOSEPH JAMES Brentford F.C Topical Times

JAMES HAGAN, Derby County F.C Topical Times.

LEONARD A. GOULDEN. West Ham F.C. Topical Times.

A selection of cards from the 1930s.

Barratt's 'Famous Footballers' (1930s).

Presented with Topical Times.

WALTER WINTERBOTTOM,
Manchester United F.C.

DAVID S. CUMMING,
Middlesbrough F.C.

GEORGE ROBINSON,
Charlton F.C.

A triple card from the 'Topical Times'.

Ardath 'Photocards' (c1936).

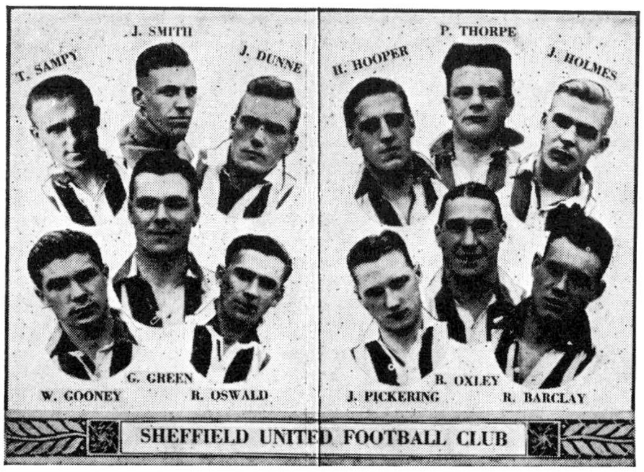

Barratt's Football Team Folders (1930s).

The Post-war Boom
The 1940s and 1950s

IN 1945 peace was restored. As in the so-called Great War, there had been massive loss of life and destruction. The war had dragged on for six long years and not only was there human loss, as with Eric Stephenson (Leeds United), who did not return, but many grounds had been taken over or badly damaged. Bombs through grandstand roofs and similar destruction meant that some clubs had to play on other grounds for a considerable period. Manchester United were forced to play at Maine Road and Arsenal at White Hart Lane. Many other grounds were taken over by bodies like the ARP for the duration and left in a shocking state.

During the war various regional leagues were formed, but the standard of football was obviously much lower than normal, with very high scores, numerous guest players and depleted teams. Various teams dropped out at different stages. Some missed most of the war, others just the odd season. In 1945-6 it was decided to operate transitional Leagues, with the top two Divisions divided into a League North and League South. In 1946-7 the situation reverted to normal, but there were still difficulties, not least because of playing staffs. Teams held the contracts of pre-war players, but, to be frank, many were now past it. Some were too old and others had not enjoyed the opportunity for regular training and matches during the conflict.

Although the anticipated resumption of cigarette card production never materialised after the war, several issues of footballer cards were made. The firm of Carreras Ltd produced, in the early post-war years, more than a dozen series on various subjects for distribution with their 'Turf' brand. These were printed in blue and white on the slides which went into packets, one picture being printed for a packet of ten and two different pictures for a packet of twenty. These sets were looked down on by collectors who remembered pre-war cards, but they had much to recommend them. The complete slides, with end and side pieces intact, are more valuable to collectors because of their virgin state, but cards cut around the frameline are certainly easier to mount in a collection.

The first football set produced for 'Turf' was 50 *Footballers* (1948). These were blue and white portraits and many older football supporters will feel a wave of nostalgia at the names and faces. Tommy Lawton, bought for a record fee by Third Division Notts County, Les Compton, brother of Denis and England's oldest debutant, Frank Swift, the giant killed in the Munich air crash, Stan Mortensen, who managed a hat-trick at Wembley. They seem like giants of the past. Of course, it was a different world then. Many were just demobbed and sported the obligatory short-back-and-sides haircut. The sudden release from the straitjacket of war, the lack of television and rival entertainments meant huge crowds up and down the country. Perhaps because of the crowds the reputations of this era seem to have lingered long and many in this series, such as Jesse Pye, Alf Sherwood, Neil Franklin and George Hardwick are remembered as greats.

In many respects the other 'Turf' series, 50 *Famous Footballers* of 1951, seems more effective. Although the first set is worth collecting, the use of dark blue on portraits leaves a rather dull impression and gives a certain lack of impact to the cards. The second series, however, contains attractive caricatures. They are well drawn and quite impressive. Scotland had a good side at the time and we can see such stars as Willie Waddell (Glasgow Rangers), Eddie Turnbull (Hibernian), Willie Bauld (Heart of Midlothian) and Willie McNaught, one of Raith Rovers' few internationals in the post-war period. Plenty of English players, like Redfern Froggatt (Sheffield Wednesday), the son of Frank, and Les Medley (Tottenham Hotspur) are also on view.

The other football 'cards' were produced for Godfrey Phillips' 'Sports' cigarettes and are reminiscent of their pre-war BDV package designs. There are two versions of these pictures to be found. The one is on thin paper, presumably cut from the soft cover of the carton, and with a blue surround. The other is printed on thick card and must have been cut from the slide. There are no other differences in the black and white photographs.

There were four sets of *All Sports* and three sets of *Footballers* issued between 1948 and 1954. As with the 'Turf' cards, the names are very familiar to older supporters and include Wally Barnes, later a commentator before his untimely death, Raich Carter, Trevor Ford, Billy Liddell, Bobby Mitchell, Roy Paul and George Robledo, one of two Chilean brothers in the Newcastle United team. Two prominent players in Scottish teams were Charlie Tully, Glasgow Celtic's Irish ball artist and wit, who sadly died in his forties, and Glasgow Rangers' Willie Woodburn, suspended *sine die* by the Scottish FA for being sent off once too often.

Although one might have expected the end of cigarette cards to have heralded the death of cards in general, this was not to be the case. There was still a great public demand for this kind of pictorial material and others stepped into the breach. Indeed, in view of the hostile opposition that has grown up towards the tobacco industry in recent decades, it may be beneficial that this happened. Certainly cards now come from more varied sources than in the early days.

Again boys' periodicals proved a valuable source of football cards, but newspapers seemed to play a more active role than in the immediate pre-war period. Many sports magazines were produced in the 1940s and 1950s and one of the best, at its height, was 'Sport' magazine. In the winter months it was mainly devoted to soccer and, amongst other things, gave all the previous week's line-ups. It degenerated somewhat in later years as it became the 'Sport Express' and eventually went under, presumably in the face of competition from the 'Soccer Star'. Around 1949-50 the publication produced a series of team groups, six lots of six stapled cards being available. Although hand-coloured, they are still good photographs and show many of the best teams of the period. We can see Huddersfield Town, for instance, with such notable players as Eddie Boot, Harold Hassall, John McKenna, Jimmy Glazzard and Vic Metcalfe.

Another series that could also be purchased through 'Sport' magazine, although it is also ascribed to the old 'Empire News' newspaper, is Mickey Durling's set of football caricatures, which was issued around 1948. Entitled the *Famous Footballers Album*, the action pictures are extremely colourful and show many of the stars of the day, including George Robledo in his Barnsley days, Len Shackleton, Roy Paul and Bryn Jones, still with Arsenal, but soon to join Norwich City. Some of the players are just names to most people today, however. These include Bill McEwan, an inside-forward from Glasgow who played for Queen's Park Rangers and Leyton Orient; Cliff Edwards, a Bristol City half-back; Joe Rutherford, a goalkeeper from Southport; and Tommy Reynolds, a Sunderland winger who later signed for Darlington. Also present is Maurice Edelston (Reading), who was an able and popular sports commentator before his untimely death. Many of the items produced at this period are already extremely scarce and often expensive. This set, for instance, is much more difficult to obtain than some of the cigarette card sets of the 1930s.

In 1954 the old Labour newspaper, the 'Daily Herald', issued a set of 32 *Footballers*. Although the backs were plain and the fronts just black and white portraits, the visual impact was quite effective and the cards are well worth acquiring. Many of the personalities are still well remembered in football circles, such as Stanley Matthews, Billy Wright and Stan Mortensen. One of the most intriguing cards is that of Charlie Mitten, for his team is given as Bogota. This was a time of enormous spectator interest, with massive crowds being commonplace, but because of the maximum wage limit imposed on professional footballers, stars like Stanley Matthews could not share in the wealth that their pulling power was generating. A small number of players left for Bogota, Colombia because of the earnings on offer, but it turned out to be a frustrating experience and all seemed to return to Great Britain in a relatively short space of time. Neil Franklin is shown in a Hull City jersey, but he had left Stoke City and an England place on this abortive adventure. Some of the other interesting inclusions are the jovial Joe Mercer with Arsenal, where injury ended his career, Ike Clarke, a Portsmouth goalscorer and 'Sonny' Walters, a winger in the Tottenham Hotspur 'push and run' side, who died in his forties.

D.C.Thomson still held a dominant place in the world of boys' magazines at this time and many a spotty youth grew up on a diet of the 'Adventure', 'Hotspur', 'Rover' and 'Wizard'. In fact the 'Rover' used to devote its front page every so often to coloured pictures of players and I can well remember cutting the pages up, so that the result looked like cigarette cards. Inserts were often given away, cards tending to be produced in blocks of four, leaving the cutting up to be done by the recipient. The quality of these cards was extremely high, both in the picture quality and biographical backs.

In 1955 a series of 24 *Famous Footballers* was distributed with the 'Wizard'. The cards, with the backs printed in orange, included players like John Hewie, a talented South African with Charlton Athletic, Len Allchurch, the lesser known of the Swansea brothers, Frank Blunstone, the Chelsea left winger and the ill-fated Tommy Taylor. The latter, who was signed by Manchester United from Barnsley for a large fee, lost his life in the Munich air crash of 1958.

In 1956 the same publication gave away 25 *Famous Footballers*, the backs this time being printed in mauve. These were colourful and well drawn, with a great impression of movement about them. At this time Wales had an exceptional side which qualified for the World Cup Finals in 1958 and present in the series are the Welsh stars Ivor Allchurch, Trevor Ford and John Charles. Ford was banned not long afterwards because of claims made about under-the-counter payments made in his autobiography. The ban was later rescinded, but by this time he was finished as a top-class player and after returning from Eindhoven he just had short spells with Newport County and Romford. Danny Malloy was a long-serving Scot with Cardiff City, who earned the nickname 'Oggie' because of his penchant for scoring own-goals. Danny Blanchflower was a great influence both with Tottenham Hotspur and Northern Ireland. Well endowed with the traditional gift of the blarney, he was later noted for a thoughtful but provocative newspaper column.

The 'Hotspur' and 'Adventure' produced a joint series of 48 *Football Stars* in 1957. These were black and white portraits with purple backs. Two ill-fated players in the series were Duncan Edwards, who eventually died of injuries sustained at Munich, and Jeff Hall (Birmingham City), who died of polio at the height of his career. There were many internationals included in the set, but a remarkable number came from teams which would now be regarded as unfashionable. Some of the performers who are in this category are Ron Staniforth, an England regular from Huddersfield Town, Jim Langley (Brighton and Hove Albion), Ronnie Clayton (Blackburn Rovers), John Atyeo (Bristol City) and Dai Ward (Bristol Rovers). In Scotland, Harry Haddock was one of Clyde's few post-war internationals. Wolverhampton Wanderers and Burnley, for whom Ron Flowers and Brian Pilkington starred, were dominant First Division outfits at the time, but have since sadly fallen into Division Four. To older football supporters it seems inconceivable. Also in the series is Malcolm Allison, later a manager, whose gift of the gab and flamboyance made him a television celebrity.

A set that was jointly issued by the four D.C.Thomson titles in 1958 was highly significant. This was 64 *World Cup Footballers* and for the first time some notice was taken of the foreign game. As has been mentioned in Chapter One of this book,

Pattreiouex's 'Footballers' (c. 1927).

Player's 'Footballers' (1928 & 1928-9).

Hignett's 'AFC Nicknames' (1933).

Ardath's 'Famous Footballers' (1934).

Carrera's 'Footballers' (1934).

Hignett's 'Football Caricatures' (1935).

Wills' 'Association Footballers' (1935).

Carrera's 'Famous Footballers' (1935).

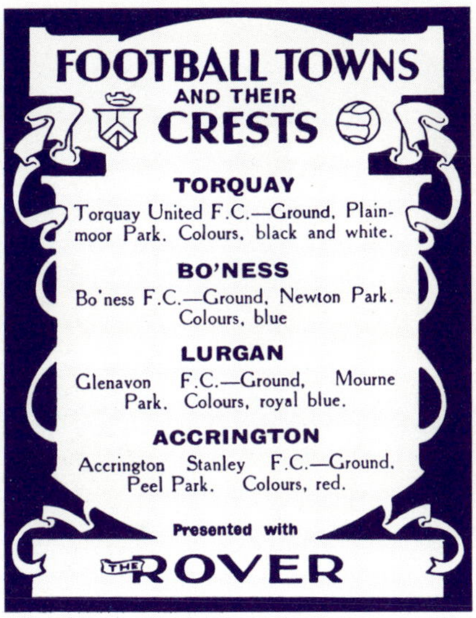

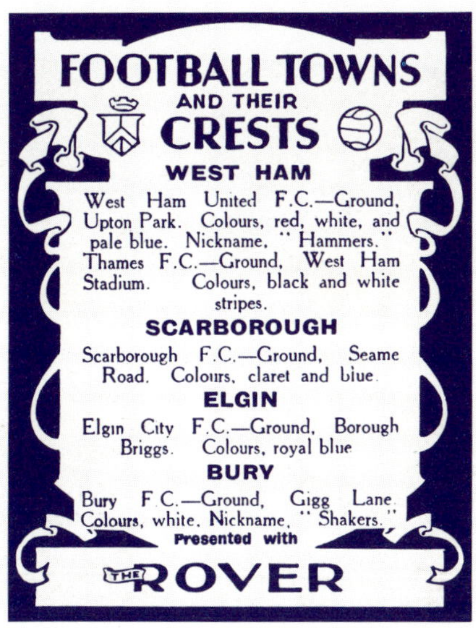

The Rover 'Football Towns & Crests' (late 1920s).

Phillips' mixed footballers (c.1936).

Ogden's 'Football Club Captains' (1936).

Carrera's 'Popular Footballers' (1936).

Wills' 'Association Footballers' (1939).

D. WELSH
CHARLTON ATHLETIC

L. J. SULLIVAN
CHESTERFIELD

B. SPROSTON
MANCHESTER CITY

C. A. FLETCHER
IPSWICH TOWN

E. M. GLOVER
GRIMSBY TOWN

G. HULLETT
PLYMOUTH ARGYLE

G. WILLSHAW
BRISTOL CITY

J. PARK
NEWCASTLE UNITED

T. LAWTON
EVERTON

S. CULLIS
WOLVERHAMPTON WANDERERS

W. J. FALLON
SHEFFIELD WEDNESDAY

R. BAINES
BARNSLEY

Hill's 'Famous Footballers' (1939).

Mickey Durlong's 'Footballers' (c.1950).

Top: Clevedon's 'Football Club Managers' (1959).
Bottom: Chix Bubble Gum's 'Famous Footballers' (early 1950).

British sides had played foreign opposition since the last century. The odd upset for England had occured in the past, but there had been an insularity about the British game. Because of their dispute with FIFA, the four home countries had taken no part in the early World Cup contests and when England eventually did take part in the 1950 competition, there was a shattering defeat by the USA. When the result came through, 'USA 1 England 0', many people thought it was a misprint and should have read 1-10. The confidence of British football was further undermined when the English team was hammered 6-3 at Wembley by Hungary, led by the master, Puskas, and proceeded to be drubbed 7-1 in the return game. There was still plenty of ability in the British game, however, and in 1958, for the only time, the four Home Countries all qualified for the World Cup Finals.

In the old days, the fame of players had spread through newspapers and magazines, and later by the odd snippet in a cinema newsreel. In the 1950s, however, the ownership of television sets became widespread, the live televising of the 1953 Coronation having given it a terrific boost. The development of the European link meant that acceptable pictures could be sent back from foreign countries. The 1954 series, in which the great Hungarian side had been thwarted, had made a big impact and there was a great feeling of anticipation before the 1958 Finals. The black and white portraits in this set give a good selection of British and foreign players.

The British players were in many cases household names. Tommy Docherty, later a controversial manager, Bobby Collins, Bobby Evans, Harry Gregg, hero of the Munich crash, Billy Bingham, the present Northern Ireland manager, Jimmy McIlroy, Dave Mackay, John and Mel Charles, Cliff Jones, Johnny Haynes, Billy Wright, Tom Finney, Jimmy Greaves, now a television entertainer. The famous names are seemingly endless, but now beside them were the foreign giants. Fritz Walter, captain of the surprise 1954 winners, West Germany, can be seen, along with Beara, the noted Yugoslavia, Gyula Grosics of Honved and Hungary and Raymond Kopa of Real Madrid and France. Viewers could now experience a sense of personal involvement as every game was shown live on a foreign pitch. Strangely, this did not signify the end of the football card. Once this had been the only way of seeing the great players, but there was still a desire to have a memento of each hero, to stick in an album or up on a wall.

In 1959 a further set was issued with the 'Wizard', this time of 44 black and white varnished portraits, entitled *Football Stars of 1959*. Some of the personalities included in the set are no longer remembered even by football followers of the time — it tends to be club supporters who remember them well. In this bracket we could include players like Bert McCann of Motherwell, Norman Hobson, the Shrewsbury Town full-back and Dave Cargill, a Scot with Derby County who made less than 100 Football League appearances.

Around three years earlier thc 'Rover' and 'Adventure' brought out an *ABC Chart of Football Colours*. This consisted of club colours on the front of a card and a cut out sheet of adhesive monochrome footballers to be stuck on the card. Not just English soccer players were included, but Scottish, Irish and Rugby League performers. All the Football League clubs are shown, so we may see players like Jim Dudley (Walsall), previously with West Bromwich Albion for ten years, Peter Hooper, with Bristol Rovers and later City, A.Campbell (Crusaders) and D.Hunter (Ards).

Apart from the 'Daily Herald' another defunct newspaper issued football cards, namely the 'News Chronicle and Dispatch'. Although these cards, issued in 1955, were known as *Pocket Portraits*, they were quite large in size (around 85 x 60mm). These black half-tone studies with advertisement backs are quite good and are arranged in clubs, which is always useful for the collector. One of the strange things is the way that some of the clubs are very easy to collect and others virtually impossible to obtain. Some of the teams, like Birmingham City, appear in all the dealers' catalogues, but others, such as Colchester United, never seem to materialise, even at auction. Some teams have famous players, like Manchester City with their FA Cup Final team including Bobby Johnstone, Bill Leivers, Ken Barnes and Dave Ewing. Others have relatively obscure performers, like Bradford City with their long-serving George Mulholland, Bill Robb and John Simm. Teams like Accrington Stanley, Peterborough United and Workington were included, along with Rugby League sides.

In 1955-6 the 'Daily Express' produced team cards for Football League sides and these were given away to spectators attending matches. Possibly these cards were issued for all clubs, but their scarcity prevents this fact from being established.

The cards produced by newspapers and periodicals made an important contribution, but sweet producers were possible even more vital in the continuation of cards. The most important contributor was once again, without a doubt, Barratt & Co. At the time of their issue these little black and white portraits of *Famous Footballers* were less prized than the host of old cigarette cards still in circulation, especially in school playgrounds up and down the country. In recent years, however, the value of these cards has shot up, with some sets going for well over £30. Possibly the reason is nostalgia, with the collectors of the time now being middle-aged, but certainly the formula of producing a new set every season was a pleasing one, even if the photographs, alas, did not change also.

The first Barratt cards to be issued in the post-war era were the *Famous Footballers* with advertisement backs. All of the subsequent series had biographical reverses. Three of these series were issued, in 1947, 1948 and 1949, but unfortunately it is impossible to distinguish between them because of the similarity of format.

Following these advertisement backed series came the 'New Series' between 1950 and 1952. The pictorial quality of these was superior to the earlier cards, which were often very dark and ill-defined. A great collection of players was to be found on these post-war cards. Take the Tottenham Hotspur contingent, for instance. This included Eddie Baily, Les Medley, Bill Nicholson (later their outstanding manager), Ronnie Burgess, Alf Ramsay (later Sir Alf of 1966 fame) and Ted Ditchburn. Others included in the series were Tommy Lawton (Notts County), George Young (Glasgow Rangers), Billy Liddell (Liverpool) and another who was to experience a tragically short career. Derek Dooley, who had begun as an amateur with Lincoln City in 1946, was, for two years or so, the most talked about name in soccer. His raw talent and physique enabled him to score 62 goals in 61 Football League games for Sheffield Wednesday. However, at the very time when he should have been approaching his peak, a broken leg quickly led to amputation. Despite his disability he has long been active in Sheffield sport and was even the Wednesday manager before suffering the uncharitable fate of being sacked on Christmas Eve.

The later series of *Famous Footballers* were numbered from A.I to A.15, the sets coming out annually. The A.1 set displayed similar types of photographs to the 'New Series', but autographs were now placed underneath and the good printing quality helped to give the cards a distinctive look. Some of the personalities shown are Tommy Taylor (Manchester United), Charlie Tully (Glasgow Celtic), Gordon Smith, the goalscoring winger of Hibernian and Arthur Milton (Arsenal), a double international at soccer and cricket.

This pattern of issue was followed by A.2 and A.3, with much the same players, but A.4 to A.7 were smaller, standard size, compared with the earlier medium-sized cards. John Charles is shown with Juventus — a sign of the times — following his £65,000 transfer from Leeds United. Quite a few Scots can be found in the series, such as Ian McMillan (Airdrieonians), George Merchant (Falkirk), Norman Davidson (Aberdeen) and the Celts Willie Fernie, Bertie Peacock and Billy McPhail. Another notable Scottish player was Tottenham's John White, a talented forward who lost his life at a very young age when struck by lightning. Some of the early Barratt series were released in Ireland by Liam Devlin & Sons of Dublin.

Various series of caricatures were created in the early post-war years, but these varied greatly in quality, both in their drawing and production. Around 1950, Kiddy's Favourites of Glasgow produced three such series and the standard was, by and large, acceptable. The cards were issued as singles, joined pairs or stapled batches and premiums were issued for complete sets. A set of 52 *Popular Footballers* was produced and this is quite useful, since it includes the national sides of the four Home Countries. Some of the players, like Tommy Lawton, Frank Swift and Neil Franklin, were household names, but others, such as Sid Thomas (Fulham), Johnny Farquhar (Queen's Park) and Dougie Sharpe (Queen of the South) are not nearly as well-known today.

The other two series were, because of the location of the firm, restricted to Scottish players. In the 52 *Popular Players* set, with three shamrocks in the design, can be found coloured caricatures of, amongst other Scots, Jimmy Mitchell, the Morton right-back, Billy Rae, the Glasgow Rangers left-half, the Stirling Albion goalkeeper Willie Archibald and Willie McGuigan, the Ayr United winger.

The 75 *Popular Players* series with five hearts in the design is similar in nature and the frequent references on the backs to World War Two help to put the cards into context and give us something of the flavour of the times. Looking at the cards we tend to think of them purely as post-war items, so it is a shock to read, for instance, that Willie Cooper had been the Aberdeen right-back since 1926. Although most of the names are pretty obscure today, there are many interesting comments on the backs which help to make the cards come alive. Charlie Watkins (Glasgow Rangers) apparently gave his greatest performance against Moscow Dynamo and Matty Lynch of Glasgow Celtic had been playing since 1935 and was currently coaching the youngsters. Jimmy Hepburn had been the Morton outside-right in the Cup Final side and Willie Laird and Tommy Adams had played for the victorious pre-war side from East Fife.

While the Kiddy's Favourites caricatures are quite reasonable, the 52 *Popular Players* (1951) issued by Junior Pastimes of Glasgow are very poor. One of the few redeeming features lies in the inclusion of now forgotten players such as Arthur Hudgell, ten years with Sunderland, Ray Goddard, who made only fourteen appearances for Chelsea, but was better known with Exeter City and Charlie Revell, the Charlton Athletic wing-half.

A series of more than 500 cards was produced by A.J.Donaldson Ltd, the printers and stationers of Glasgow. The set was drawn by John Barr, who spent his life working in the Clydebank shipyards before emigrating to Australia in his seventies (in 1983). Not only footballers were included, but boxers, speedway riders, snooker players and so forth. This is really a composite set, but can be broken down basically into two main parts, namely the 'big heads' and 'wee heads'. The former, consisting of 90 cards, were issued between 1948 and 1950. The 'wee heads', including this first 90 redrawn, were produced from 1950 to 1953. These were apparently sold in stapled blocks of eight for 3d.

Because of the Glasgow connection the set had something of a Scottish bias and present are such characters as W.Fraser, the Third Lanark goalkeeper, T.Brawley, the Cowdenbeath centre-half and 'Doc' Fitzsimmons, the Clyde right winger.

Many of the trade sets from this period are very scarce and one particularly so is the series of *Smashers*, issued by Sport Photos of Glasgow. These are black and white photographs of Scottish footballers, such as the Glasgow Celtic great, Bobby Evans.

The firm Chix Confectionery Co Ltd of London was well-known to schoolboys of the 1950s, who had to purchase large quantities of unpalatable gum in order to obtain the outsize cards (around 96 x 51mm). The first series of 48 cards was produced in

1951, the first 24 being drawn and the second being the distinctive Chix colour photographs. Among the stars to be seen in this set were the fiery centre-forward Trevor Ford; the 'Clown Prince of Soccer', Len Shackleton; and 'Wor Jackie' Milburn of Newcastle fame.

The remaining two series consisted entirely of good quality colour action photographs. In the second set appeared, amongst others, the ill-fated Manchester United trio of Roger Byrne, Duncan Edwards and Jackie Blanchflower. The latter, Danny's brother, escaped death, but was so badly injured that he could never play again. This set came out in 1952 and the following year saw the issue of the third set, which included Jimmy Melia, later manager of FA Cup Finalists Brighton and Hove Albion, a young Jimmy Greaves and Ollie Norris, a well-known Third Division personality with Bournemouth.

A strange set of 48 *Footballers* was produced by Chix in the late-1950s. The cards had a bit of everything, for on the front was a portrait and action shot of the subject and on the reverse a caricature and biography. Among the players to receive this treatment were Bill Perry, always remembered for the 1953 FA Cup Final, John Atyeo, whose 597 Football League games for Bristol City yielded 315 goals and Phil Woosnam, the Welsh international later involved with the North American Soccer League. Shown in a Norwich City jersey is Terry Bly, a prolific goal-scorer who played a key role in Peterborough United's first Football League season, 1960-61.

Some sets from this period, such as the 25 *Popular Footballers* produced by W.R.Wilkinson & Co Ltd of Pontefract, are rarely seen, but others, like those of Cadet Sweets, Slough, Sweetule Products Ltd of Manchester and London, Mitcham Foods Ltd of Mitcham and Kane Products Ltd of London and East Grinstead are all on dealers' lists and can be purchased quite cheaply.

Cadets produced two sets of 50 *Footballers*, in 1957 and 1958. The cards are unusual in so far as the backs are printed upside down compared with the fronts, the idea being to flip them over. Portraits and action pictures are included and the overall quality is good. Some well-known personalities were illustrated on the cards, amongst these being Bobby Robson, the present England manager and a fine footballer himself, Don Howe, Jimmy Greaves, Brian Clough and Bobby Charlton. Kane's set of 25 *Football Clubs and Colours* (1956) can be obtained very cheaply, but their 25 *International Football Stars* (1957), including such players as Barschandt of Austria, is rather more expensive.

The majority of sets follow the same tried and tested path, so that it is always a pleasure to find a set that is different and the subject of some thought. In 1959 Clevedon Confectionery (Blackpool) Ltd produced a series of 50 *Football Club Managers* and, strangely enough, this seems to be the only occasion it has ever been done. The set, now quite rare and valuable, was put out in two versions, one with a blue, the other with a mauve surround, but there are no apparent differences in content.

This set obviously includes many men who had enjoyed long and interesting careers in football. Jimmy Anderson, for instance, of Tottenham Hotspur had originally joined the club in 1913. The illustrious Bill Shankly was with Huddersfield Town and it goes without saying that Matt Busby was with Manchester United. Some of the personalities enjoyed considerably more fame as players than as managers, such as Sam Bartram of York City, but many did have long and distinguished careers in managerial posts. These included Cliff Britton (then with Preston North End), Jimmy Trotter (Charlton Athletic), Harry Catterick (then with Sheffield Wednesday, but better known with Everton, where he died at a match), Joe Mercer (Sheffield United), Alec Stock (Leyton Orient), Ted Drake (Chelsea), Vic Buckingham (West Bromwich Albion), Scot Symon (Glasgow Rangers) and Ted Bates (Southampton). Others, although not managers in the top flight, were well-known at a lower level, and these included Billy Lucas, three times in charge at Newport County, and Dave Russell, with Bury and later Tranmere Rovers.

Two attractive and useful sets were issued with 'Soccer' Bubble Gum, produced by Merrysweets Ltd. These were two series of 48 coloured *Soccer Teams* (1957 and 1958), quite large (around 97 x 51mm) and with the team members identified on the reverse. The real pity is that not all the Football League clubs were included, for these are effective sets in format and content. Some teams actually appear in both series, but with different photographs and team groups.

The 1957 set includes some teams from the lower echelons of the Football League, such as the late, lamented Accrington Stanley (not the present non-League side of the same name), Hartlepools United, Chesterfield and Wrexham, with their Welsh international forward Ron Hewitt. The famous 'Busby Babes' are there and the photograph shows, amongst others, Eddie Colman, Duncan Edwards, Roger Byrne and Tommy Taylor. Wolverhampton Wanderers had an illustrious side with Billy Wright, Jimmy Mullen, the schoolmaster Dennis Wilshaw and numerous others and Aston Villa also had a fine side, which included Peter McParland and Jackie Sewell.

The second set was equally interesting and amongst the lesser lights shown were Darlington, Brighton & Hove Albion, Workington, with the ex-Sunderland South African Eddie Purdon, Stockport County, Southport, where the great Stan Mortensen was ending his career, Scunthorpe United and Northampton Town, with the Welsh goalscorer Ken Leek. Ipswich Town were a more modest outfit than in recent years, though with some able and long-serving players, such as John Elsworthy and Roy Bailey.

A firm which has played a gradually more important role in card production since the 1950s is known in the catalogues as A & BC. This is the American and British Chewing Gum Ltd, a subsidiary of Topps (USA). The first set of interest was issued in 1954, 100 black and white cards known as

All Sports. This set is very rare today and is already in the £100 bracket.

The first purely football sets issued by A & BC were two batches of 46 *Footballers* distributed in 1958. These were quite large coloured portraits. The pictures were pretty poor in their reproduction, though the biographical backs were good. The real significance, however, lies in the fact that they were the first of many, for the firm has since issued football series at regular intervals and has become one of the cornerstones of modern production. The personalities in this first series seem to be a mixture of old and new. People who have made an impact on modern football are there, such as Bobby Robson, Don Howe and Don Revie, as well as players more connected with the immediate post-war era, such as the Blackburn Rovers full-back Bill Eckersley, Ted Ditchburn and Tottenham Hotspur's Channel Islander, Len Duquemin.

Cards have come from some very varied sources and one set of easily obtained footballers came in 1952 with the popular table football game 'Subbuteo', marketed by P.A.Adolph of Tunbridge Wells. At first two separate sets of 24 matt *Famous Footballers* were brought out, then an extra two cards were added and a set of 50 glossy cards issued. Some famous and very talented internationals are shown in the series, like John Charles, Danny Blanchflower and Peter Doherty, at the end of his career with Doncaster Rovers. Even with the Rovers he was still capable of scoring 55 goals in 103 Football League games. Other players were well-respected on a slightly lower level. These included Sid Gerrie, a one-club man who had six years with Hull City, Frank Bowyer, similarly loyal and the scorer of 138 goals in 398 League appearances for Stoke City, Andy Graver, who had three spells with Lincoln City, and Gladstone Guest who, in nine years at Rotherham United, scored 130 goals in 356 games.

An equally unexpected source of football cards was the National Spastics Society, which in 1957 issued a set of 24 small (70 x 38mm) *Famous Footballers*.

In 1948 Hull City produced a set of 20 bright cards of their playing squad. These quite large items, which were issued with club programmes, are quite sought after and formed one of the few sets produced by a club. The players appear in their black and gold strip and good accounts of their careers appear on the reverses. At the time the illustrious Raich Carter was the Hull City manager and another interesting inclusion was Viggo Jensen, a Dane from Skagen who spent eight years with the club. Three particularly well-known personalities were goalkeeper Billy Bly, a Hull City institution who died in 1982, Eddie Burbanks, one of Sunderland's FA Cup winners of 1937 and the Scottish wartime international Willie Buchan, who shortly afterwards left for Gateshead. Other players are now less well-known, like Norman Fowler, an ex-schoolboy international full-back who left for Gateshead at the same time as Buchan.

Some other sets issued in the 1950s include 25 *Football Caps and Badges* (1958) by F.Lambert & Sons Ltd, the tea firm of Norwich and the much scarcer 25 *International Footballers of Today* (1955) by Reddish Maid Confectioners of Stockport.

Various non-card football items are seen from time to time. In the 1950s, for instance, the 'Rover' brought out two booklets, the 'Pocket Guide to Football League Colours' and the 'Handy Album of Famous Football Jerseys'. These well-produced, coloured albums did not just comprise the Football League clubs' strips of the time, but the colours from bodies like the Corinthian League, Birmingham League and Kent League.

In 1948-9 the 'Sporting Mirror', a fairly short-lived publication like 'Sport' magazine, produced two sets of lettercards, strips of photographs similar to those that can be bought at seaside resorts. These lettercards were restricted to the London clubs. One consisted of 12 *Famous Soccer Stars*, including players like Ronnie Rooke, Arsenal's tough-looking centre-forward and Ted Ditchburn of Tottenham Hotspur. The other comprised six *Famous Football teams*. The players were listed and we can see, for instance, Arsenal's notable team of the period, with the Compton brothers, Joe Mercer, George Swindin and Bryn Jones.

Around the late 1940s various booklets of black and white photographs were sold. These were packed with pictures of footballers and football teams and can still be bought very cheaply, often for a pound or so, as is the case with a series of brochures entitled 'Football Favourites'. To take another example, 'Soccer Snapshots', issued in 1949, was sold for one shilling at the time. Some of the performers are just obscure names today and similar photographs of them could only be located with the greatest difficulty. These include Ernie Edds, a Plymouth Argyle centre-forward, John Meaney, who played 288 Football League games for Crewe Alexandra, Eric Lancelotte, a Brighton & Hove Albion inside-forward born in India, Walter Kealey of Accrington Stanley, Bill Lee (Barrow) and Alan Middlebrough, whose fame lay in 47 League games for Rochdale.

From these booklets something of the atmosphere of the time comes across. These were the days when no-nonsense, robust centre-forwards could still barge long-suffering goalkeepers over the goal-line. A case can be made that the 1950s saw the end of 'British' football. The introduction of the protected, continental goalkeeper and the clamping down on the more physical aspects of the game over the years has seen the traditional British game develop into something different. Sadly, the new restrictions have not always bred more artistry, but often a more negative game.

As in earlier periods, card production was not solely confined to Great Britain. In 1951-2, for instance, an anonymous set of Belgian team photographs was produced. These black and white cards showed teams like Racing Mechelen, FC Liégeois and OC Charleroi.

In the early 1950s the Munich firm Austria G.m.b.H. produced two series of 'Bildwerk' issues entitled *Konig Füssball* (King Football). These were broken down into sub-sets of 25 cards, which could be obtained by collecting a specified number of coupons. These large (116 x 81mm) black and white photographs showed, amongst other things, match action from the Kaiserslautern v Stuttgart German Cup Final and shots of well-known German internationals, such as Helmut Rahn, Maxi Morlock, Jupp Posipal and Otmar and Fritz Walter. Scenes from the 1952 Germany v Ireland international can be viewed, with people like Con Martin in action.

The firm also issued a set of 100 cards in 1954, entitled *Deutschland — Füssball-Weltmeister* (Germany — World Champions).

By the late 1950s cracks had begun to appear in the inbuilt belief in British superiority. It was no longer a case of foreigners trying to compete on British terms, but of British teams trying to compete on the same terms as the best foreign sides.

An anonymous set of Belgium team photographs issued in 1951-2.

Six of the Manchester United stars who perished at Munich, from a News Chronicle set issued in the mid-1950s.

Above: Watford footballers from a set produced by a local newspaper in the late 1950s. Below: Barratt's 'Famous Footballers'.

RON STANIFORTH

DANNY MALLOY

DOUG HOLDEN

GEORGE ROBB

HARRY GREGG

HARRY HADDOCK

BOTELHO JULINHO

FAY COYLE

GORDON SMITH

JIMMY O'NEILL

TOM JOHNSTON

JEFF HALL

D.C.Thomson Footballers from the 1950s.

Modern Times
From the 1960s to Date

THE 1960s saw the rebirth of hope for British football. After various thrashings, especially at the hands of the Hungarians, England at last won the World Cup, which they had at one time ignored, and they achieved the feat in front of their own fans. British teams also began to do well in the newly instituted European competitions, notably Glasgow Celtic (1967) and Manchester United (1968) in the European Cup, and Tottenham Hotspur (1963) and West Ham United (1965) in the European Cup-winners' Cup.

Boys' magazines still produced quite a few series of cards, but there was a definite change. Gone were much-loved titles like the 'Adventure' and the 'Wizard' and the old serious reading comics were gradually phased out in place of comic strip types, particularly with the influence of television, which stressed the visual image at the expense of the written word.

Among the publications which gave away cards in the 1960s were 'Victor', 'Hornet' and 'Hurricane'. Some of these sets were, in fact, very interesting and different from similar material in the past. Various plastic wallets were issued with black and white photographs of an intriguing collection of teams. One would not have expected, for example, to find pre-war teams in a set designed for boys.

'Victor', one of D.C.Thomson's later titles, gave away 22 extra-large (125 x 80mm) black and white photographs known as *Star Teams of 1961*. Mainly soccer sides are included in this series, although the Wigan and St Helen's Rugby League sides are shown and the national Rugby Union sides. There is an interesting collection of soccer sides, such as Linfield, Walsall, just promoted from Division Three, Dunfermline Athletic (manager Jock Stein), Glenavon, Kilmarnock and Crystal Palace, who had the Welsh international goalkeeper Vic Rouse, 'Budgie' Byrne and John McNichol, who made over 100 appearances for three clubs, Brighton & Hove Albion, Chelsea and the Palace themselves.

Another Thomson title, the 'Hornet', issued a series entitled *Top Teams of Today and Yesterday*. These large (220 x 154mm) items included two teams per card. The coloured strips of team groups and individual photographs showed, amongst other things, Morton, Dundee, the 1964 Scottish FA Cup Finalists with Andy Penman and Alan Gilzean, the well-known West Ham United side of John Bond, Bobby Moore and Geoff Hurst and a FIFA Select XI (1963), which featured Ferenc Puskas, Lev Yashin, Uwe Seeler, Raymond Kopa, Denis Law, Alfredo di Stefano, Eusebio and Gento — a great side indeed.

Various sets were put out by the D.C.Thomson titles at this time and all were quite interesting. The 'Victor' series *Cup-Tie Stars of All Nations* illustrated three players per card and included a fair balance of British and foreign stars. Amongst the personalities to be seen were Ron Flowers, Jim Baxter, Alex Elder, Gento, Sekularec, Pele and Joe Baker, who made the full England side despite playing for Hibernian.

The Sportsman's Wallet, *Famous Teams in Football History*, had a photograph of the ill-fated 1958 Manchester United team, with Roger Byrne, Mark Jones, Eddie Colman, Duncan Edwards, Tommy Taylor, Liam Whelan and the talented outside-left David Pegg, who was aged 22 when he died at Munich. The selection of teams is particularly interesting, with the 1960 Real Madrid side, the 1927 Cardiff City FA Cup winners, the 1953 'Matthews' team of Blackpool and the successful 1959 Norwich City underdogs, with McCrohan, Ashman, Allcock and Terry Bly.

Famous Teams in Football History, an extra large (138 x 84mm) series given away by 'New Hotspur', held an intriguing collection of antique sides, such as the first Wembley winners (Bolton Wanderers, 1923), the Everton 1930-31 side and the 1939 FA Cup team of Portsmouth. Also to be seen is the shock side of 1961-2 — Ipswich Town, who won the First Division championship under Alf Ramsey.

The 48 *Stars of Sport and Entertainment*, issued by the 'Hotspur' and 'Rover' were old style black and white portraits and consisted of a mixture of entertainers and soccer stars, such as Tom Johnston, who scored well over 200 goals in his career before emigrating to Australia.

Fleetway Publications Ltd, of London, issued a few football related sets with its magazines. 'Hurricane' gave away *Star Footballers of 1964*, for instance, 40 coloured pictures on yellow or brown backgrounds of players such as Frank Wignall, Ron Clayton and Burnley's Irish international Alex Elder.

Around this time Buchan Publications produced a series of distinctly average coloured cards, which were similar in style to the first A & BC issues. The IPC magazines 'Lion' and 'Scorcher' gave away strips of coloured portrait and action pictures and, no doubt, various similar football sets can be found by digging through catalogues and reference books.

National newspapers have produced various sets of cards over the period we are reviewing and most have been well worth collecting. Clearly, newspapers have easy access to printing and to journalists with the necessary knowledge of the game. Circulation figures are all important, not least because of the need to attract advertising, and these sets have been employed to try and attract the sports-minded reader.

In 1970 the 'Sun' brought out a medium-sized (69 x 51mm) set of 134 *Football Swap Cards*. The big drawback with this series is that no captions are to be found on the cards giving details of the individual players. In addition, with some of the larger squads players are so small as to be indistinguishable.

While these 'Sun' cards are a big disappointment,

a set produced by its rival, the 'Daily Mirror' managed to bring the concept to fruition. The set of 100 *Mirrorcards* was produced in two versions, the normal issues being standard-sized, but with much larger premium issues entitled *My Team* being available. The cards were made available in the 1971-2 period in exchange for vouchers printed in the newspaper. They were coloured and well produced and included the 92 current Football League sides, the four national sides and various Cups. Because of the degree of coverage they give to the contemporary football scene they are an extremely useful addition to any card collection.

The *Mirrorcards* are reminiscent of some pre-war series (eg. Ardath) in their panoramic scope and it is worthwhile to sit down and really study the cards. Some of the teams of the time have gone downhill. Crystal Palace were in their heyday at this time with players like Alan Birchenall, who spent fifteen years in League football, Steve Kember, with almost 500 Football League appearances in his career, and Bobby Tambling of Chelsea fame. Barrow have since dropped out of the League, as have Southport, with their impressive 14-stone forward Eric Redrobe, and Workington, with the craggy full-back Joe Wilson, who later emigrated to Australia.

The Irish national team includes Bob Lutton, who only made 42 League appearances in a three-club career, and in the Sunderland side Jim Montgomery, always remembered for his fabulous Wembley save, and Ian Porterfield, now the manager of Aberdeen. These two players starred in the team's FA Cup Final defeat of First Division Leeds United, a memorable performance. The Arsenal team was an impressive one, with stars like Bob Wilson, Charlie George, George Graham and the great servant George Armstrong, but the Manchester United side included some unusually obscure names. On the Manchester card can be found players like John Connaughton, who made only three appearances for the Reds, but was later a regular for Port Vale, Willie Carrick from Dublin, who only ever made four Football League appearances and Bill Watson, who played just eleven games in the League.

In 1975 the 'Sun' introduced an interesting concept with its *3-D Gallery of Football Action Stars*. 50 cards were produced and the attempt to use new technology was to be welcomed, but unfortunately many of the photographs were uninspiring. The use of training grounds and empty stadia gave a distinct lack of atmosphere to the cards. Some of the personalities in the series were Terry Venables, now manager of Tottenham Hotspur, Alex Stepney, for eleven years the Manchester United goalkeeper, and Tony Currie, an England midfielder with a terrific shot. Another series issued by the newspaper entitled *3-D Gallery of Football Stars* also used the technique.

In 1980 the 'Sun' produced a set of 1,000 *Soccercards*. The set was broken down into seven sub-sections, such as *International Stars* and *All Time Greats*. The set was criticised at the time for its lack of quality and errors to be found in it. This cannot be said of the recent 'Daily Mail' series, however, which is excellent in quality and likely to be sought after in the future. Many cards in this particular set contain two small coloured photographs, but there are larger cards.

Some of the more interesting characters to be found in the 'Daily Mail' series are Osvaldo Ardiles and Ricardo Villa, Tottenham Hotspur's popular Argentinians, Peter Borota, Chelsea's somewhat eccentric Yugoslav goalkeeper, the same team's giant centre-half Mickey Droy and the impressive coloured full-back then of Nottingham Forest, Viv Anderson.

The cards we have mentioned so far all come from national newspapers, but the odd series has been issued from time to time by more local newspapers. One set which is not seen very often today was produced by the 'West Herts Post' around 1960. Twelve black and white photographs (81 x 50mm) of *Watford Footballers* were given away. In those days, well before the advent of Elton John, the team was one of the lesser lights of the Football League. The best-known performer was Cliff Holton, who in more than 500 League games scored nearly 300 goals. Sammy Chung spent seven years with the club, as did the ex-youth international Freddie Bunce.

The 'Manchester Evening News' is fortunate in having two such prominent teams to cover. In 1976 30 pictures of City and United players were produced, with five large sheets (83 x 62mm) containing six pictures each. Both teams at the time had not only fine footballers, but characters as well. Rodney Marsh, a very talented footballer, made regular appearances on the television screen, Asa Hartford is still involved in the lower levels of the League after more than sixteen years, Colin Bell was an incomparable England midfielder, whose career was damaged by injury, and the irrepressible Lou Macari is now a successful manager with Swindon Town.

In the early 1970s the 'Scottish Daily Express' issued 24 *Scotscards*, which showed some of the notable Scottish personalities of the day, such as Bob Wilson, Lou Macari, the midfield dynamo Archie Gemmill, the Manchester United captain Martin Buchan and Jimmy Johnstone, often dismissed from the pitch because of his fiery temper.

Amongst confectionery firms, Barratt & Co Ltd has held a prominent position in the distribution of trade cards, as it has done consistently since the 1920s. Although the company was taken over by Geo. Bassett & Co Ltd in the 1970s, it has retained its own identity as the Barratt Division. Since 1960 many different series have been issued, but all have held to the formula that characterised the 1950s issues of the firm — standard-sized cards on the theme of the *Famous Footballer*.

The last of the *Famous Footballers* sets issued in the 1950s was A.7. A further eight sets were issued, the final one being A.15 in 1967 and all consisted of 50 cards. All of these sets have rocketed in price, even A.10 which was always cheaper than the others because remainders were sold off to dealers. The sets were coloured, but unfortunately many were poor in quality and are certainly inferior in that respect to many of the firm's black and white sets. The idea of using autographs was retained and this gives many of the Barratt sets a characteristic quality.

Since the A.10 series is rather more easily available than the others, it may be useful to look at some of the personalities to be found there. The sadly deceased Gerry Hitchens is pictured with Internazionale — there was something of a football drain to Italy at the time, with Jimmy Greaves, Denis Law and John Charles heading in that direction. Although Gerry's early career was spent with Cardiff City, he was an England international, having been born in Kidderminster. Ted Phillips' ability to find the net helped Ipswich Town in their early rise to prominence, for he grabbed 160 goals in his ten years with the club. Terry Paine, a well-respected citizen who later became a JP, had time not just to make 709 League appearances for Southampton, but to play over 100 times for Hereford United in their early League days. Two fine footballers whose careers were terminated in a bribery scandal were Peter Swan and Tony Kay (Sheffield Wednesday), and another talented player shown in the set is the Stoke City left-back Tony Allen, twelve years with the club and three times an England international.

Various players appear in more than one series and some random examples of players to be found in these later sets are George Hudson, a prolific goalscorer in the lower Divisions, Alan Suddick, who spent ten years with Blackpool, Dave Burnside, a noted ball-juggler with West Bromwich Albion and Gary Talbot, a press photographer who was persuaded to play professional football for Chester and Crewe Alexandra.

Although the title *Famous Footballers* was abandoned after A.15, much the same format was retained for later series. In 1974, for instance, a set of 50 *Soccer Stars* was issued. One disadvantage with this particular set is that some of the cards are horizontal and others vertical. This is a bugbear for collectors who like to house their cards in albums of one sort or another, as most do.

In 1974 a set of 50 *World Cup Stars* was produced. In recent decades Scotland have been more consistent than England in reaching the World Cup Finals and the Scottish squad was the only British one to qualify for the 1974 Finals. Quite a number of the Scots have since done extremely well in managerial careers and among the blue shirts we can see players like Lou Macari and George Graham (Manchester United) and Kenny Dalglish, then with Glasgow Celtic. Some other famous Scots there are David Hay, Peter Lorimer with the thunderbolt shot and Danny McGrain, always associated with Celtic's European success.

The players with other nations were obviously the cream of world football and the names have quite a ring to them. Amongst others we can see Gerd 'Bomber' Müller, the German goalscorer, Franz Beckenbauer, the 'Kaiser', and the incomparable Johann Cruyff of Barcelona and Holland.

Virtually every year sees a further issue of Barratt-Bassett footballers. The general standard of these cards is good — indeed, they are much better than the earlier coloured efforts of Barratt. To give an example, *Football 1981-82* is a pleasing collection of portrait and action pictures, where we may glimpse such contemporary heroes as Gordon Strachan (Aberdeen), Sammy Lee (Liverpool), Alvin Martin (West Ham United) and Glenn Hoddle (Tottenham Hotspur), an outstanding midfield player whose talents have often been overlooked by England. 'Football' is now the up-to-date name of the series, but in style and content the cards are little different from the old *Famous Footballers.*

One firm which we have previously mentioned is Clevedon Confectionary Ltd. Although the firm was not a major producer of cards, it had a knack of putting out attractive and imaginative little issues. In 1961 a series of 50 *Famous Footballers* was produced. These coloured caricatures featured a mixture of the famous and obscure. Foreign performers such as Raymond Kopa (Real Madrid), G.Boniperti (Juventus and Italy) and Alfredo di Stefano (Real Madrid and Spain) were to be found, as well as English players like Stanley Matthews. Also present, however, were players who even in their own day were relatively obscure. These included Mike Tiddy, a right winger who spent most of his League career with Cardiff City and Brighton & Hove Albion and Mervyn Jones, who played for Scunthorpe United, Crewe Alexandra and Chester.

Dandy Gum, a Danish firm situated on Velje, produced a set of 210 *Football Clubs and Colours of the World.* Although the idea was good, with brief details of different countries' teams on the backs, as well as the illustration of their colours on the fronts, the pictures were decidedly uninspired. Instead of known footballers, boys were pictured in the colours and the photographs appeared to be taken in the middle of nowhere.

The same firm produced a set of football playing cards in 1986, given away with 'Football' Bubble Gum. Many of the players to be found in the series are well-known thanks to the recent World Cup Finals in Mexico. Platini and Tigana (France), Socrates (Brazil), Laudrup (Denmark), Blokhin (Russia) and Maradona (Argentina), scorer of a controversial, but decisive, handled goal against England, are all fresh in the memory, as are British players, such as Gary Lineker who was the leading goalscorer in the competition. As the years go by, however, these players will become simply old memories, just like the old World Cup heroes, Fritz Walter, Ferenc Puskas, Pele and the others.

The 1958 set of A & BC has been mentioned and since then the firm has become, like Barratt & Co, a mainstay of modern football card production. So many sets have, in fact, been issued that it is impossible to cover them all here. For any collector who is interested enough, a reference book has been compiled purely of the card issues of this firm. Most of these series are known simply as *Footballers* (there are literally dozens) and the majority follow the well-worn formula of a collection of famous players. The cards are almost all quite large and various sets have been devoted purely to Scottish personalities. The similarity of format is to a great extent indicated by the fact that reference books refer to the colour of the backs to identify the different series.

While the majority of A & BC sets are very similar, the odd one turns up which shows more invention. In 1970, for instance, 36 *Real Photos of Footballers* came out. The cards had deckled edges, which is itself unusual, and the fronts showed black and white photographs with blue autographs superimposed. The players which were featured include Peter Osgood, Francis Lee, Joe Royle and the speedy Liverpool winger Peter Thompson.

Some of the non-card issues are difficult to find. For instance, in 1966-7 the firm gave away not only cards, but players' portraits printed on thin paper. The pictures, which were folded over into four, showed players like Jimmy Greaves and George Cohen. One set of particular interest comprised the sixteen teams of the 1970 World Cup Finals. These were very large coloured team groups, with the national flags also being illustrated. There are some names to conjure with. Yehoshua Feigenbaum (Israel), Benkhrif Boujemaa (Morocco), Murtaz Khurtsylava (Russia). How they roll off the tongue. It is valuable to have such team groups. If only we had similar photographs of the contestants in earlier World Cups.

The fact that the more conventional issues of A & BC have been glossed over is in no way to disparage them, for they form a very valuable body of cards, from an historical viewpoint, having covered British football continuously since the late 1950s. Many of the cards contain good quality colour pictures with instructive biographical notes and the coverage given to Scottish sides is especially welcome. To take just one example, in the purple-backed Scottish series we can find players such as Stan Rankin (Morton), John McHugh (Clyde), Henry Hall (St Johnstone) and John Martis (East Fife), performers we would be unlikely to see in any other series.

Since the 1960s football cards have been issued by all sorts of companies, from PK Chewing Gum to Tonibell Ice Cream, and they have come in all sorts of shapes and sizes. In 1960 another confectionery firm, Dickson Orde & Co Ltd of Farnham, produced a set of 50 *Footballers*. These cards, like the later Barratts, are standard sized (62 x 36mm). They are cheaply priced and well worth acquiring. The coloured pictures are good and an interesting collection of players is contained. A remarkable number have had managerial careers, for instance Bobby Robson, Brian Clough, Ronnie Allen (West Bromwich Albion), Peter Taylor (Middlesbrough), Ian Greaves (Manchester United) and Bob Stokoe (Newcastle United).

A product in a completely different field that has been involved in issuing football cards is Sumner's Typhoo Tea. The Typhoo brand has been the source of different kinds of material. Most people must have seen their package designs, which were produced from the mid-1950s onwards. Series devoted to football were *Famous Football Clubs* (1962) and a second set the following year, *International Football Stars* (1964) and a second series in 1969. These designs were printed lengthways on the side of the packet and had to be cut away.

These package designs have their limitations, as with the 'Turf' issues, but much more prized are the premium cards which could be obtained from the firm. Again four football series were produced, *Famous Football Clubs* (1964) and a second set the following year, *Football Stars* (1973) and *International Football Stars* (1969). As with the packet issues, all the sets contain 24 cards. These premium issues are beautifully produced, being very large coloured pictures on fairly stiff board and certainly the team photographs are almost worth framing. Some of the sides to be found in the series are Cardiff City, with John Charles, Derek Tapscott and Ivor Allchurch, Leeds United, with their Welsh goalkeeper Gary Sprake, Jackie Charlton and the fast, coloured winger Albert Johanneson, and Rotherham United. Many of the teams appear in both series, but with different photographs. The set of *International Football Stars* has facsimile autographs and both sets of team and individual photographs are well worth collecting.

A firm which produced some pleasing little pictures was Top Sellers Ltd of London and Leicester. Long series entitled *Football* were issued each season from 1972 to 1977. Portraits and action pictures were used, as well as team badges, composite pictures and some caricatures of players like Beckenbauer and Pele. Conventional coloured photographs of personalities like Kevin Hector, the Ipswich Town South African Colin Viljoen and Trevor Francis, then in a Birmingham City jersey, were to be found among the sets.

Nabisco Foods of Welwyn Garden City, the successor to the Shredded Wheat Co, produced a series of 24 quite large *Footballers* in 1970. These were reasonable coloured portraits, although certainly Bobby Charlton and Denis Law look in pain on their respective cards. Shredded Wheat issued a series of very large cards entitled *Champions of Sport*, which included Danny Blanchflower, Jimmy Greaves and Bobby Charlton and the firm has since produced a set of *Footballers* which seemed to be aimed at a fairly juvenile audience.

The firm of J.Lyons and Co has issued two series of football cards with its 'Lyons Maid' brand of ice cream, namely 40 *International Footballers* (1972) and 40 *Soccer Stars* (1971). These are now fairly scarce and expensive. The *International Footballers* are attractive coloured action shots. It is interesting that the 'continental' ball with its different coloured panels can be seen. This is different not only to the traditional ball, which contemporary British spectators were accustomed to, but also to the old segment ball that can be glimpsed on some of the earliest cigarette cards. Some British performers, like Ron Davies, Billy Bremner, and George Best can be seen in this set, as well as a good selection of foreign players. The latter include Eusebio, Pele and Beckenbauer, in addition to more obscure players of the calibre of Mordecai Spiegler (Israel), Gustavo Pena (Mexico) and Hector Chumpitaz (Peru).

The *Soccer Stars*, which have green backs, include names well-known to older supporters. Alun Evans (Liverpool) was a useful player and two extremely gifted performers were Charlie Cooke, the Scottish international who made more than 200 appearances for Chelsea, and Don Rogers, the flying winger who played more than 400 times for Swindon Town, but could have gone much further if he had joined a bigger club.

In the last ten years many good football series have been produced and they continue to be issued regularly. The firm FKS Publishers Ltd of London, for instance, has produced numerous football sets for sale in packets and these have carried titles such as *The Wonderful World of Soccer Stars* and *Soccer.* The cards have been issued since 1968 and the number in each set has tended to be large. To take just one example, in 1978 the firm put out a set of superb coloured team photographs called *Soccer Stars.* The drawback with these cards, which were intended for a 'Trump Card Game', is that they have no captions giving players' names. With the top English clubs of the time, like Leeds United and Manchester United, this does not present much of a problem, but this is not the case with foreign sides. Nevertheless, this is a set well worth obtaining, with its quality photographs of teams like Juventus, Feyenoord, Benfica, Barcelona and Real Madrid.

The firm of Prescott-Pickup has also produced various series in recent years, for instance with its *Famous Footballers* of 1979. These action portraits show the likes of the Scottish star Archie Gemmill and the pint-sized Welsh regular, Brian Flynn (then with Leeds United.) Top Trumps have issued a variety of football series, normally restricted to one club per set, and Topps Chewing Gum Inc produced large (in size and number) sets of *Footballers* from 1975 onwards, most of them having a Scottish and English edition.

A quite attractive series of 36 *World Cup Stars* was given away by the potato crisp manufacturers Golden Wonder in 1978. Argentina won the Cup before its own fans and amongst the players shown are the talented Mario Kempes, who was the leading scorer in the competition, and Daniel Bertoni. Other sets have also been issued by this firm.

Some of the best card issues of recent years have come from the firm of Panini, situated at Modena in Italy. The amount of effort put into the Panini cards is fantastic. Not only does the Company issue sets in Great Britain and Italy, but even in countries like Belgium, Egypt, Turkey and Greece. The picture quality is very high and the number of cards per set is high. Apart from odd series which have been produced, eg. for World Cups, a regular set of *Football* has been produced each year since 1978. Every one of these contains over 500 cards. While it is impossible to describe every series, it may be helpful to discuss a few random sets.

Panini cards are all coloured and the 1978 British series consists mainly of individual portraits of First Division performers. With Leeds United we can view players like Trevor Cherry, Tony Currie, Joe Jordan and Eddie Gray. In the Liverpool squad we can glimpse 'Crazy Horse' Emlyn Hughes, Ian Callaghan, Steve Heighway and John Toshack who, after taking Swansea City to the First Division, was sacked and went to manage a Continental side. Bristol City, in their heyday before the old club suffered liquidation, mustered performers such as Peter Cormack, Norman Hunter, Gerry Gow and Trevor Tainton. Smaller Scottish clubs only enjoy brief careers in the Premier Division and walk a knife-edge between professional and part-time status. It is significant that Ayr United, who are featured in the series, had lost various players by the end of the season. Joe Fillipi, ex-Coventry City, had gone to Glasgow Celtic, Rikki Fleming to Hibernian and Mike Larnach to Motherwell. Some interesting individuals are included in the set and one we can spot is Johannes Edvaldsson, the Icelandic captain who was on Glasgow Celtic's books.

Among the following year's cards we are again confronted with some interesting squads. In the Bolton Wanderers side we can see a young Peter Reid, the talented Willie Morgan and Frank Worthington, who fairly recently was sacked by the Administrator appointed to run ailing Tranmere Rovers. Southampton had Ivan Golac, from Partizan Belgrade, Alan Ball and the able goalscorers Ted MacDougall and Phil Boyer.

Panini have used a successful formula of giving individual pictures of English First Division and Scottish Premier League sides and team groups for Division Two. If there is one criticism to be made, it is regarding the team groups. The players of the Second Division sides are not named and, since the series already run to more than 500 cards, it seems churlish not to include team groups of Third and Fourth Division outfits.

Among the 1984 cards can be seen stars of a newer generation, such as Charlie Nicholas and Tony Woodcock of Arsenal, Norman Whiteside and Gary Bailey of Manchester United, Gary Birtles and Ian Wallace of Nottingham Forest. Notts County, then in the First Division, had a distinctly cosmopolitan look with Tristan Benjamin, born in St Kitts, the Nigerian John Chiedozie and the Algerian international Rachid Harkouk. Dundee United, once the whipping boys of Scottish football, were now established as one of the top sides, with players of the calibre of David Narey, Eamonn Bannon and Paul Sturrock. The whole range of Panini cards has been consistently good and it is well worth investing in a new set every year, for the numerous cards in every set increase in historical value with the passing of time and are likewise likely to increase in financial value. The attitude of the firm is shown by the fact that a card museum has been opened in Modena.

One unique set, which is unfortunately unlikely to find any competition, was issued by F.M.Dobson Ltd in conjunction with the 'Evening Chronicle' in 1982. It was entitled *Newcastle and Sunderland's 100 Greatest Footballers* and it is what it claims to be. The only drawback is that these black and white portraits were printed on very flimsy paper, but the whole history of these two great North-Eastern sides is contained in the series.

Amongst the great Newcastle United stars are Bill McCracken, Colin Veitch, Stan Seymour (later the club chairman), Jackie Milburn, Hughie Gallacher and Malcolm Macdonald. The heroes in red and white shirts include Ned Doig, Charlie Thomson, Raich Carter, Trevor Ford, Brian Clough and Jim Baxter. These cards have a great historic quality about them and if similar sets had been produced for other areas, the bonus would have been great indeed.

Another area to benefit from recent coverage is Plymouth. Two sets have been devoted to Plymouth Argyle and the 1983-4 issue is of particular interest, as that was the season the Third Division side reached the FA Cup semi-finals. The set is entitled *The Pilgrims' FA Cup Squad 1983-84.* The large black and white caricatures, with green shirts, show manager John Hore and his side, which includes the evergreen Tony Kellow, who now manages to combine playing with running the Exeter City Social Club, and the fiery Tommy Tynan, a player who has been known to be overzealous even in practice games. Sets of this nature really reflect local pride in a team.

This chapter has been mainly concerned with cards, but various odd items have been produced, in many cases by petrol companies and sometimes in conjunction with competitions. Esso, for instance, created a set of 22 coloured player portraits on circular pieces of metal (diameter 38mm). Current internationals like John Toshack, Martin Peters and Malcolm Macdonald were included and the items were given away in paper packets which themselves had players' pictures printed on the inside.

In 1970 a 'World Cup Collection' was distributed, consisting of 30 aluminium coins of England players, such as the Charlton brothers and Bobby Moore OBE. Another set of aluminium coins (diameter 27mm) was produced to commemorate the Centenary FA Cup Final, the 1972 game between Leeds United and Arsenal. Thirty coins were created for previous winners of the competition, but the earlier Old Boy winners and the like were ignored.

Other items of interest were produced by Esso. A set of 76 adhesive club badges were given away and these were designed to be stuck into an album. Sixteen 'Squelcher Booklets' were given away to customers. The idea of these was to 'squelch' or put down arguments and these quite small booklets (80 x 53mm) contained a mixture of facts and coloured pictures. The booklets were on different topics. Number Three, for example, contained the World Cup Story and included pictures of players like Uwe Seeler (West Germany) and Riva of Italy.

Other related items can be found, such as the 'Sun's' series of *Football Stamps*, and, although any collection will consist mainly of cards, these miscellaneous bits and pieces tend to add a little variety.

The period covered in this chapter has been a turbulent one in the history of British soccer. It has seen high points, such as the 1966 World Cup victory and very low points, such as the senseless fatalities in the Heysel Stadium. Not only this, but a vast number of changes have taken place. The introduction of the Football League Cup, artificial pitches, sponsorship, substitutes, the abolition of the maximum wage, protection for goalkeepers, the increase in foreign and coloured players, these are just a few that come to mind. Some of the changes have been mirrored in the cards produced, for instance, in the players' strips. Certainly many of the happier moments can be recalled by seeing the pictures of Bobby Charlton, Bobby Moore, Georgie Best and many, many others.

Many people have tried to write off soccer, but it remains the leading winter sport. It is significant that football cards have been used very recently in an attempt to boost some newspapers' circulation. The 'Sun', at the beginning of 1987, started giving away vouchers for Panini football cards. The vouchers came out for a week and, on the receipt of six free cards, the reader was left to buy the other 500 cards for himself! The 'Daily Mirror' gave away vouchers for its own specially designed cards. This offer lasted for four weeks, but, unfortunately, after Week Three the cards seemed to be unobtainable at any newsagents. Whatever the limitations of distribution, the events showed that football had not lost much of its pulling power.

The early cigarette cards are now strictly historical items. Each supporter comes into the sport at a different point, supports different teams and, because of this, a collection is a very personal thing. Every generation demands its own heroes. Every new game pushes previous ones into the past, and every debutant means that another player is on his way out of the game. It seems strange to the supporter of ten or twenty years ago, but already Bobby Charlton, Denis Law and Georgie Best have passed into the history books, along with 'Nudger' Needham, G.O.Smith and Billy Meredith. The players have gone, but, thanks to cards, the memory lingers on.

J. E. Doig
(Sunderland)

Hughie Gallacher
(Newcastle United)

Trevor Ford
(Sunderland)

Malcolm Macdonald
(Newcastle United)

F.M.Dobson cards, issued in conjunction with the Newcastle Evening Chronicle, from a set portraying 'Newcastle and Sunderland's 100 Greatest Footballers'.

Useful Publications & Addresses

For anyone interested in purchasing cigarette or trade cards, there are many dealers around, some big and some small, some who specialise and others who just have a few sets of cards amongst numerous other items. For a long time the two foremost firms in the trade have been:

The London Cigarette Card Co Ltd
Sutton Road
SOMERTON
Somerset
TA11 6QP

and

Murray Cards (International) Ltd
51 Watford Way,
LONDON
NW4 3JH

Various other quite large firms can be found in the Press and at the numerous antique fairs that seem to be held up and down the country these days there are usually some old cards to be found. Not only cards themselves can be obtained, but reference books and accessories, including the modern plastic albums that help to show off collections.

The Cartophilic Society of Great Britain Limited is the leading collectors' organisation, details of which can be obtained from the London Cigarette Card Company. The latter firm produces an excellent little magazine known as the 'Cigarette Card News and Trade Card Chronicle' and the Cartophilic Society the 'Cartophilic Notes and News'.

Anyone interested in the history of football is recommended to contact:

The Footballer
72 St Peter's Avenue
CLEETHORPES
Lincolnshire
DN35 8HU

Over the years soccer has suffered greatly in comparison with cricket when it comes to coverage in serious books. In recent times, however, the situation has greatly improved. Excellent histories of many clubs have been compiled, particularly those in the highly-acclaimed Breedon Books 'Complete Record' series. Another welcome development has been in the issue of various Who's Who books which have been devoted to different clubs. Probably the biggest influence has been Douglas Lamming. His Who's Who books on England (completed with the late Morley Farrar) and Scotland are being reissued and he has also brought out books on Grimsby Town and Hull City. Other authors have written similar books on their own teams, and hopefully many more will do so in the future.